Midge
On Her Own

By
Mildred Thompson Olson

TEACH Services, Inc.
PUBLISHING
www.TEACHServices.com • (800) 367-1844

World rights reserved. This book or any portion thereof may not be copied or reproduced in any form or manner whatever, except as provided by law, without the written permission of the publisher, except by a reviewer who may quote brief passages in a review.

The author assumes full responsibility for the accuracy of all facts and quotations as cited in this book. The opinions expressed in this book are the author's personal views and interpretations, and do not necessarily reflect those of the publisher.

This book is provided with the understanding that the publisher is not engaged in giving spiritual, legal, medical, or other professional advice. If authoritative advice is needed, the reader should seek the counsel of a competent professional.

Copyright © 2005 TEACH Services, Inc.
ISBN-13: 978-1-57258-340-5 (Paperback)
Library of Congress Control Number: 2005926898

CONTENTS

	Preface	v
Chapter 1	Rites of Passage	1
Chapter 2	High School—Here I Come	7
Chapter 3	Testing Times	15
Chapter 4	Camping with Indians and Saints	25
Chapter 5	Dorm Rules—Bah! Humbug!	33
Chapter 6	Metamorphosis	43
Chapter 7	On My Own	55
Chapter 8	Living in the President's City	61
Chapter 9	College? HO! Wedding? NO!	77
Chapter 10	Making Major Changes	91
Chapter 11	At Union College	105
Chapter 12	The End of the Year	123
Chapter 13	Bikes, Books, Bulls and Witches	131
Chapter 14	Practicing Professionalism	151
Chapter 15	1 + 1 = 1	167

PREFACE

I was filled with great expectations as I entered my teenage years. I soon discovered, however, that life was not all fun and games. Frustrations multiplied as serious decisions had to be made. I could not have fathomed then the far reaching effect those choices would have upon my character and future life.

In high school I was torn between being popular and being a Christian. Problems involving Sabbath observance, worldly friends and pleasures, and other enticements kept me yo-yoing between the forces of good and evil. Although my parents and my church family were not on hand to encourage me through the day-to-day crises, I drew strength from what they had taught me in my younger years.

After graduating from secondary school, I took the bus to Washington, D.C., to seek my fortune. I didn't have the money to go on to college, but I was so anxious to get an education that I was willing to leave home and work in order to accomplish that goal. In Washington, I learned about the pleasures, thrills, and the whirl of activity that constitutes life in a metropolis. I found good employment, saw the sites, enhanced my cultural knowledge, began college, and made friends. The good things, however, were counterbalanced by frightening, complicated situations—an attempted burglary in the house in which I stayed, a murder I witnessed, and an engagement I broke. The Christian path I had intended to walk had become so cluttered with my work, social life, and education that it obscured my childhood goal of becoming a missionary.

After two years, I returned to the midwest and Union College where other challenges awaited me—finding my niche in life, working my way through college, writing for the city newspaper, and choosing a profession and a life companion.

Some opportunities in life seem to come about as a result of being in the right place at the right time. Getting the job at the college store and writing for the paper fell into that good-fortune category. I believed, however, that these good things happened to me because God was in charge.

The summer colporteuring in Minnesota among the Swedes and the Germans rewarded me with excitement, satisfaction, and a scholarship. What could be more stimulating than meeting a genuine witch with supernatural powers or being chased by a bull?

Out on my own, I was thankful to have God help me make my decisions. Those choices culminated in a happy marriage and the prospects of achieving my life time dream—to become a missionary.

CHAPTER 1

RITES OF PASSAGE

I was twelve years old and tired of being referred to as "the baby in the family." Youngest, maybe, but not BABY. Sometimes when Mom got particularly nostalgic, she would say something like, "Pass the potatoes, Baby." I knew she was talking to me, but I was tempted to respond, "Babies can't pass potatoes," or "I don't see a baby at the table."

I was, therefore, very pleased when our family had a population explosion. Dick Thompson was born to my brother Nels, Marlin Bakke to sister Martena, and Bob Combes to sister Jean. The birth of these three nephews when I was 12 provided my rite of passage. With so many real babies around, my family was forced to give me a new status. At last they recognized my chronological maturity.

That summer I was urged into another rite of passage, my spiritual transition. One Sabbath after church Pastor Stanley, who was in his late seventies and becoming quite feeble, approached me. "Mildred," he said, his deep wrinkles cracking only slightly around the corners of his mouth, "it is now time for you to be baptized."

I jerked to attention. "You still do that?" I asked in astonishment, quite certain that the wizened old saint no longer had the strength to lift a person out of the water. Fears of drowning gripped my mind. "I don't swim, you know," I warned him.

"Yes, we'll do it in the swimming pool at Madison," he answered, picking up on my word "swim". I should have talked louder. I knew he was becoming quite deaf.

Since he hadn't caught my real concern at all, I pressed for reassurance. "But, ah, <u>you will do it at the shallow end of the pool</u>—where I can stand up—won't you?" I sincerely wanted to be baptized, but I also wanted to survive.

"School?" he questioned, not really hearing me at all. How could he mistake "school" for "pool" except that his mind was focused only upon giving me information. "Yes, yes, we'll have Sabbath School and worship with the Ash Grove and Madison churches. Then, after our potluck dinner in the park, we'll walk over to the pool for the baptism. Besides you, there will be Betty and Harold Flatten, Thelma Otter, and others."

"Si-six or s-seven kids?" I stuttered, unable to believe that Elder Stanley would choose this sacred rite upon which to test his strength. I had come to revere this old man who had been our pastor for so many years. I didn't want him to drown himself or us.

The baptism took place as scheduled. We candidates were embarrassed, however, when the swimmers were asked to vacate the pool and wait while we were baptized. Some of them resented our intrusion, while others ridiculed the religious ceremony they did not understand. All of this detracted from the sacred aura that I had imagined surrounded a baptism. My decision to serve God was serious, but the surroundings were not. Elder Stanley did a creditable job, though we had to help ourselves up by splashing our way to the surface.

RITES OF PASSAGE

I moved on into my seventh and eighth-grade school years. Those were the two years of elementary education that South Dakota students dreaded because of the state's stringent two-day testing program. If we did not pass their standardized tests with a score of 75%, we had to repeat the whole year. Some students in our county repeated the grade several years, while others simply dropped out of school at that stage. So Betty, my only classmate, and I really crammed for the ordeal. We made it through the seventh grade tests easily. The next year, after we finished the State's tests, we congratulated ourselves. We knew we had passed.

In June we got the results from the county superintendent's office. Along with our scores came the invitation to attend the graduation ceremonies for Moody County eighth graders at the courthouse in Flandreau. That Saturday night there must have been more than 100 candidates lined up for graduation. On cue, we marched in to the front row seats, pledged allegiance to the flag, squeaked through the "Star Spangled Banner," and sat through the superintendent's boring speech. When our names were called, we walked to the platform to receive our diplomas. It was a mass, impersonal ceremony with one exception—those who had maintained an average of 90% or higher in all subjects were given special recognition. I was elated when they called, "Mildred Thompson, high honors." Thus, I had successfully completed another rite of passage. Since my sisters Lela and Gladys had previously graduated with honors, my psyche couldn't have stood getting anything less. I had always competed with those older sisters. It seemed they were the best in everything. I, the youngest in a family of eight, followed in big footsteps; but I was determined to stretch those foot prints—to be something or do something that the others had not.

I could hardly wait to begin high school so that I might accomplish something—anything. I didn't know where my talents lay; I'd been hunting for them a long time. I remained optimistic, however, because I believed that every bell had a clapper that gave it its special ring. I wanted my clapper to start sounding. I wanted to be as good as, yet different from, my sisters. I needed to feel I was an original—not just a reproduction of someone else.

I was anxious to begin high school for another reason. That summer my parents grew an enormous garden. From it we canned half-gallon jars full of corn, green beans, beets, and carrots for Plainview Academy. Gladys wanted to attend the academy her senior year, so the academy agreed to take produce in lieu of the cash we did not have. What Gladys would earn working at Plainview Academy, along with our produce, would pay her expenses for the year.

We never worked so hard in our lives as we did that summer. Our backs ached constantly from bending, hoeing, and picking produce from the garden. We often got burned lifting the big jars from the hot water bath in Mom's copper boiler. On top of that, we had to gather the cobs and wood fuel for the cook stove. No education was bought with more hard labor or family effort. It was a proud day for all of us when Julius loaded the last of the canned goods and Gladys into his pickup and drove off to Plainview Academy.

What galled us girls the most was that Dad had earned enough money that summer threshing grain to have paid cash for Gladys' education. But one of our Adventist members wouldn't pay the threshing bill he owed Dad. The man argued, "I have to send my daughter to the academy, and if I pay you, I won't have the money. So you'll just have to wait, Martin."

Gladys and Lela stand above Midge in a family portrait.

Dad tried to explain that he had the same problem—that Gladys, now a senior, wanted to attend the academy, too. But the member reneged and said he would never pay Dad the bill if he asked for the money again. Then Lee stopped attending church causing the first rift among our church family. That made all of the members feel badly. It made me sad, too, but only on Sabbaths. During the rest of the week it made me plain mad. Dad was so forgiving! And that made me twice as mad. I felt my sisters and I were paying the price of the unpaid bill. Dad must have guessed how I felt because one day he explained his reasoning to us girls:

"I know you girls resent Lee's not paying me what he owes me. And not paying a bill for services received is dishonest. However, sometimes it's better for a Christian to accept what is and not fight for what should be. I could take him to court, but that would cost both of us money and neither of us could send our daughters to the academy. Further, it would not make Lee feel better towards me or the church. First Corinthians 6 says we are not to take a brother to court. So, if he never pays me, we will manage without his money. God will bless us as He always has. So, let's forgive and forget."

Dad walked away leaving me with a guilty conscience. Sometimes I wished Dad didn't have Bible texts to clench his points. Quoting scripture ended my desire for debate. The Bible was the final word in Christian ethics as far as our family was concerned. Dad was right, as usual. Gladys got to the academy in spite of our lack of cash.

The man never did pay his debt, but we forgave him and were blest. Years later, my parents and my brother Julius succored this man and his wife in their poverty and welcomed them back into the fold. Julius willingly transported Lee and his wife to the doctor, church, store, etc. They needed love, help, and sympathy. While Dad and Julius had prospered, even purchasing the farm on which my father had spent his first winter in America in a dug-out soddy, the Lees had failed financially.

Dad, however, never considered his material comforts important. He believed his greatest assets were his eight, faith-filled children. Through Dad's example I learned that forgiving spells PEACE. Grasping this spiritual concept was another rite of Christian passage for me.

CHAPTER 2

HIGH SCHOOL—HERE I COME

The year Gladys was a senior at the academy, I entered high school as a freshman. I was ready and raring to go! I hoped that some high school teacher could discover my latent talents. I believed I must have at least one.

More important to me than fame or fortune, talents or grades, was a social life. The first day I looked over all of the freshman girls, trying to decide who among them would become my special friends. I noticed that there were two sisters and another girl who began the year with a flare of popularity. That's where it's at, I thought. I will get in with those girls. So I edged my way into this crowd, but I never felt very comfortable. The girls smoked, drank, and were worldly-wise. I figured I could put up with this unacceptable behavior and still not become a part of it. Besides, we four girls did a lot of things together that were innocent and fun.

One evening the sisters had a party at their house. Of course, I, their special friend, was invited. They served ham sandwiches which I didn't eat, beer which I didn't drink, and cookies which were my main course. They played cards which I didn't play, gambled which I didn't do, and got very familiar with the boys which embarrassed me. I felt like the prodigal who, when he came to his senses, wanted to return to his father's home. I wanted only to get out of there. I knew I was in the wrong crowd, but I had wanted to be with these popular girls.

MIDGE ON HER OWN

The blessing came when they didn't want me to be with them.

The Monday after the party, I noted a chill in the girls' attitude towards me. I ignored it. They walked in a close threesome, leaving me to trail along behind. They talked to each other in soft voices, snubbing my every effort to become a part of the group again. I even bribed them with my black walnut fudge. That lasted only until the last morsel melted in their mouths. By the end of the week, I knew I was getting the brush-off. I accepted my fate.

The next Monday morning I returned to school with a heavy heart. I had lost my friends and needed to get new ones. That was not easy since half of the school year was over. When everyone left the assembly hall for the lunch room, I remained in my seat. I had no special friends with whom to eat lunch. I put my head down on my desk wanting to cry; I felt frustrated and lonely. Then I heard gentle sobbing on the far side of the huge assembly hall. I looked across the room and discovered it was Helen, another freshman girl. She too was alone. I wondered who had been Helen's best friends, and if they had deserted her as I had been cast aside. I activated my courage and went over to her. "What's wrong, Helen? Is there anything I can do?"

She looked up at me through tear-brimmed eyes. "Well, yes, Mildred, there is. (They called me Mildred in high school.) Algebra is easy for you, isn't it?"

It was, as a matter of fact. I always got top grades in the class and Helen knew it. But since mother had drilled into us children that humility was a Christian virtue, I tried to act virtuously. "Yes, I do all right in algebra," I admitted, not concealing my pride very well. "Why?"

"Because I just can't work these problems. I need help before class."

"But, Helen, I thought you were a straight-A student. You graduated with honors when we got our eighth-grade diplomas at Flandreau."

"That was before this section of algebra. That's what kills me! I've always had A's. Now this algebra is ruining my G.P.A. I hate it!"

"Hate is a pretty strong word for my favorite subject, isn't it?" I laughed. "But I'll help you with algebra if you'll help me with Latin. I dislike it!"

We struck a deal. I explained algebra to Helen, and she helped me conjugate my Latin verbs. For the next month, Helen and I often spent the noon hour helping one another. It paid off. I became an A student in Latin, as did Helen in algebra. Our names were always on the honor roll, whereas my former girlfriends were barely passing any class. Helen and I soon had lots of spare time. The teachers allowed us to do our homework for the next day in class while they explained the lessons to the other freshmen. Helen and I were scholars, not just students; we wanted to become professionals, so we applied our efforts to learning all we could about everything.

Helen and I had other things in common. She was a Christian of the Lutheran faith and encouraged me to become a missionary for my church. Our Danish/German parents were farmers and quite pleased that Helen and I had become friends.

"Water seeks its own level," Mother philosophized. "So I'm glad you aren't running with those other girls anymore. You'd soon be down in the slough with them. They were popular, but they didn't have good morals and goals. Their worldliness and unhealthy habits would have ruined your spiritual and physical life. You, as a Christian, have a responsibility to the people of this world. You are supposed to make life better for others. The girls you were running with ridiculed those who were poor or came from certain families, weren't as intelligent or well dressed, or had weird personalities. Making fun of those who are different only drives them into worse despair. It is amazing how early in life children begin picking on the odd ones. That's the time when Christian parents and teachers need to stop this harassment. We can make a difference in their lives by treating the unaccepted with genuine Christian friendship."

"Mom, that's good philosophy, but it just won't work," I argued even though I knew disputing her would bring on a longer sermonette. "I want respectable friends, not weirdos or jerks."

"Right. But by ridiculing or ignoring the weirdos you make them more weird. And the jerks act stupid to get your attention. The jerks and weirdos need acceptance. For one week you knew what it felt like to be rejected; just think how the odd ones feel being rejected day after day. How would you like to walk in their shoes?"

"Well, I got new friends. They can too."

"No, they can't," Mom disagreed. "They feel so worthless that they don't have the courage to try. They have no self esteem."

"Well, what do you want me to do?" I was disgusted with this dialogue. I knew I didn't want to be associated with the odd kids.

"I want you to do what Jesus would do. Be merciful and kind to everyone. For those who are loners, just a casual greeting in the hallway isn't enough. Break up your group some days, and each of you spend time with them. You might be surprised how interesting those weirdos are. Remember Jesus says, 'Blessed are the merciful, for they shall obtain mercy.' It takes mercy on the part of Jesus to accept us as we are. So we need to do the same for others. In the judgment day God isn't going to ask you if you were popular or important in the world; He's interested in what you did to help people. In the end, you'll be happy that you helped make a difference in people's lives. May God help you, Midge. By the way, you'll always need good associates like Helen, so keep close to her. You'll be happier with Helen as your friend."

Come to think of it, I was already far happier and relaxed now that Helen was my friend. I was no longer water seeking a lower level. I didn't have to pretend to enjoy the things those other girls did. My conscience was celebrating the change. Now if I could just apply the "be merciful" part....

I don't know just when Hilda joined us, but she was a blessed addition. She was always cheerful and brought a little sunshine with her wherever she went. Virginia, daughter of the telephone operator, also joined our group. We four had lots of good times during the noon hours, and we didn't need beer, cigarettes, or dirty stories to do it.

We began our sophomore year in good spirits. But just a few months into the school year, Virginia got nephritis, an incurable kidney disease. I prayed that God would heal her miraculously as He had me when I had ruptured my appendix. Helen, Hilda, and I visited Virginia every noon break to buoy up her spirits. But the visits did little to lift our anxiety. Hopes for her recovery dimmed as her disease progressed. We watched her grow weaker. Her twinkling brown eyes lost their luster and seemed to sink into their sockets. Her skin turned yellowish and her frame gaunt, but Virginia continued her brave struggle for life. As her strength failed, she at last had to accept the fact that death would be her fate.

The last day we saw her alive, tears trickled down Virginia's hollow cheeks. "I don't—want—to die," she gasped. "I'm too—young. I want—what—you have—health."

I turned away, trying to blink back tears. The sniffling sounds coming from the other side of Virginia's bed made me know that Helen and Hilda were having as much trouble handling the situation as I was. So the four of us gave vent to our emotions and had a good cry. It was cathartic—we were now better prepared to accept the inevitable.

The day Virginia died, and the days that followed, sobered us high school students. It forced us to realize that youth has no guarantee against the grim reaper. We were destructible.

Some of the boys in our class were pallbearers, and the service included nice tributes from Virginia's friends. But there is nothing nice about the death of a 15-year-old friend. It hurts—a lot! It was a long time before I could have fun without feeling an empty ache deep inside of me. Somehow it didn't seem right for me to be enjoying life while my young friend lay in the grave. I prayed that God would take away this pain, and gradually He did.

Time mended the fragmented pieces of my heart and pushed me along the continuous ebb and flow of earthly life—the mundane and the spectacular, the ordinary and the extra-ordinary. So far high school had not been the complete satisfaction that I had expected it to be. I hoped that better days would lie ahead.

Hilda and I joined the musical organizations. Helen and I joined the debate team. I joined almost all the other organization possible, including the drama class, and the basket and softball teams. I would have joined the band too, but I didn't have the $25 to buy an instrument. I wasn't the best in any of the organizations, but I surely had a lot of fun. I was never a soloist for our autumn operettas, but the chorus members got to wear costumes and that satisfied me. I wasn't good enough to be on the first line-up of the ball teams either, but just being a substitute excited me. I filled in on the debate teams, wrote skits for assembly, or acted in a drama. Just being involved gave me incentive to go for the top.

"Why can't you just be satisfied with what you can accomplish, and forget what you can't?" Mom chided. But I couldn't do that. I wanted a big piece of the action and decided that I could make it happen my junior year.

CHAPTER 3

TESTING TIMES

My junior year I arrived. I was in the center of all the school activities and thrilled to be there. First I was chosen to be a member of the girls' sextet, a special choral group that sang for community gatherings. I was very pleased with this honor, never suspecting that it might be accompanied by problems. I was blithely enjoying this degree of success when I ran into a testing time. Our sextet was asked to sing for a Friday night community gathering. Now I had a conflict with Sabbath observance. I knew what I should do, and I did it. I went to the principal, who was also the choir director, and told him that my parents wouldn't let me sing on Friday nights.

"And why not?" he bellowed, his eyes flashing signals of irritation. "This is a public relations affair for Colman High School, and we will sing."

"But my parents, ah, are, ah, we are Seventh-day Adventists," I gulped.

"So?" Mr. Stevens stared at me, waiting for a better explanation.

"Well," I hesitated, trying to find the right words. "My folks won't let me sing worldly songs on Friday nights." Somehow it seemed easier to make my parents responsible for an unpopular decision. Mr. Stevens eyed me as if he had never seen me before. I hastened to explain further, "Sabbath begins at sundown on Friday night, ah, that is, ours does. So, ah, my folks won't let me..."

"That so? Well, I'll just phone your parents right now and explain the importance of this engagement," he said, picking up the phone. In a minute he had Mother on the line. I wished I could have heard Mom's end of the conversation, but all I was getting were the principal's arguments. His used-car-salesman approach didn't sound very reassuring to me. Mr. Stevens hung up the phone and turned to me. "Your mother says that you can do whatever you like, that you are old enough to make you own decisions regarding religion."

"D-did my mother really say that?" I gasped in disbelief. He nodded. How could she do this to me, I wondered? Why didn't she bail me out of this awkward situation? Didn't she know it would be easier for me if she said no? Did she really not care what I did?

"Well, what about it?" Mr. Stevens demanded. "Give me your answer now so that I will know if I must replace you. I hope you will sing, however. You know all of the songs, and you six girls' voices blend the best. I don't really want to replace you. But if I must, I must. I don't think God would mind if you sang just this once. Then from now on I'll try not to accept Friday night engagements."

That day in the principal's office I faced a decision that could make a difference in the direction my life would take. Would God care if I broke the Sabbath just a little? If I didn't sing, would I lose my place in the sextet? I had become quite popular with the other students. Would the kids think I was a religious fanatic if I chose not to sing?

On the other hand, to whom did my loyalties belong—to man or lo God? He gave His life to redeem me, and all He asked in return was my love and loyalty. How could I let Him down? Others of His children had passed more serious testing times than this. Martyrs had given their lives. Mr. Stevens cleared his throat.

"Just a minute, Mr. Stevens, I need to think this through," I said, turning my back to offer a quick prayer. God and Jesus were still sitting up there on their golden thrones, just as I had envisioned them as a child. But I couldn't see that either of them were making a move. I felt that both were waiting anxiously for my decision. God and Jesus were not telling me what to do, and neither were my parents. The rite of passage into adulthood included self-direction. I knew that the decision would be mine alone, and that I would have to live with the consequences. I knew too that whatever decision I made would either weaken or strengthen my spiritual life. I was experiencing the great controversy between Christ and Satan within me.

Turning to this big man, whom I dearly loved and respected, I said, almost inaudibly, "I'm sorry, Mr. Stevens, I cannot sing tonight."

"I'm sorry too," he responded, quite audibly. "You made a poor decision."

I ran from the principal's office to the girls' cloakroom and cried. Would Hilda and Helen forsake me for my religious convictions like the three girls my freshman year? Perhaps. I had to take that risk. I would rather lose the popularity and success I had gained thus far than to disappoint Jesus.

I waited for the weekend to be over. I was anxious, yet I dreaded, to go back to school on Monday. Ours was a small school—less than 100 students—so news traveled fast. Although all of the students knew that I was a Seventh-day Adventist, I wasn't sure they could appreciate the stand I had taken for the Sabbath. They didn't keep Sunday the way I kept Sabbath. On Monday I would feel their response to the choice I had made.

Since the Nebbin girls—Hilda, Annette, and Laura—rode to school in the same car service as I did, I figured I could get a hint of what was ahead of me for the day from their attitude. They greeted me in their usual jovial manner, and I breathed a sigh of relief. But would it be the same with the rest of the students? Though God was my best friend, I wanted flesh-and-blood friends whom I could touch and with whom I could talk.

I was quite apprehensive as I entered school that day. Almost immediately I was aware that the other students knew of my decision to keep the Sabbath holy. But instead of avoiding or deriding me, they actually seemed more friendly than usual. No one referred to the incident directly, including Mr. Stevens who said casually as he passed me in the hallway, "You're still a member of the sextet."

I learned from the other members that the sextet had sung that Friday night with just five girls. None of the next performances were scheduled for Friday nights, so we remained a complete sextet.

That same year there were two performances of the operetta—one on Thursday night and the other on Saturday night. I could conscientiously take part in both. Had Mr. Stevens arranged it that way for my sake, even though I didn't have a lead part? I secretly felt that he had.

That fall I was catcher on our soft ball team. When winter came, I was chosen to be a substitute on the A-string basket ball team. In spite of my short stature, I had speed. My jumping ability made me an acceptable guard. When we won a game, I knew the credit belonged to my team mates, but I still liked being one of the gang on the sports team.

Julius took me to all of my games and gave me moral support by yelling encouragement from the sidelines whenever I was on the floor. One Friday afternoon we were playing against Chester High School. They grew a lot of giant-sized girls in Chester. The forward I guarded was nearly six feet tall. I was leaping into the air during most of the game, just to be on her level. This drained a tremendous amount of energy from me. Suddenly I collapsed to the floor, unconscious. I awoke as they carried me off on a stretcher.

A doctor was called to examine me. He determined that I had a heart problem—a leaky valve. He told Julius and the coach that I should never do excessively strenuous exercise such as basketball. I was disappointed because I now had to drop out of sports. Further diagnosis confirmed the suspicion that my heart problem was the result of rheumatic fever—a complication from the mastoid infection I got from a snowball injury to my skull during my second grade year.

School still held a lot of fun for me, and it was all happening my junior year. I was active in the drama, debate, and journalism clubs, besides the music organizations. Miss Berthoud, my beloved English teacher, got me started writing and speaking. She was the best! She taught Latin, English, drama, debate, speech, and journalism. I took all of those classes. She was an older lady, all business but extremely brilliant and inspiring. I tried to emulate her in every way. I knew now that teaching English would be my profession.

I also admired Miss Berthoud's dedication to her church. She was a devout Catholic and attended mass every morning. (Perhaps every teacher needs a shot of religion before beginning a day with teenagers.) In any case, I figured there must be something very special about the Catholic Church to captivate my heroine's devotion. It was with some intrepidation that I informed my mother of my interest in Catholicism. She was so shocked at my admission that she couldn't speak at first. Finally she regained her composure. "Go investigate, and you will see that they don't teach everything that's in the Bible."

I couldn't believe Mom was right. I went to talk with the priest to learn what the Catholics believe and why. He wanted to study only from the catechism, while I insisted that we learn only from God's word, the Bible. "Well," he said, slapping the catechism closed, "you are already in the only church that teaches all of the Bible truth. The other Protestants follow many of our teachings. For instance, we changed the holy day from Saturday Sabbath to Sunday. And we had the right. We get our doctrine from the successors of the disciples—the Popes. Their communiques from God are more recent, therefore more accurate and obligatory.

Our encounter ended pleasantly even though we disagreed. He held to the popes and the catechism, and I stuck with the Bible.

Miss Berthoud was still my favorite teacher. She started me writing news notes about the school for our town's weekly paper, THE COLMAN ARGUS. I even got a by-line. I think my parents were proud to see my name after the articles I wrote, though they seldom mentioned it. Lela and Gladys had both done some writing too, so I wasn't the first in the family to explore this medium. Eventually, writing became a hobby for me.

I thoroughly enjoyed writing and speaking. I wrote and directed short plays and skits. I told stories, gave readings, and delivered speeches for class, assembly, and any other occasion. Participating in the interscholastic debate contests gave me more opportunity to hone my speaking skills. Florence Kruger was the best of our school's debaters. I usually teamed up with her in favor of the issue. Florence always took the last rebuttal, clinching the victory with her final, most convincing arguments. Our school won a trophy that year, thanks to Florence's quick repartee.

On the debate team was a sophomore boy, Leo Lellelid, who was a gifted debater. He was a sincere Lutheran Christian who wanted to become a minister and then become a missionary. We developed a close friendship and dated. We went to ball games and social events and on music and debate trips. We picnicked, roller skated, and boated together. We encouraged one another to go for awards and medals.

During the spring I entered the speech contest, I had done so the year before and had won second place. Betty Flatten, my grade school classmate and church friend, won first place. This was a blow to my ego, since I had usually topped her in everything before. I had to admit, however, that Betty had done the better job of interpreting her reading. Though I was glad for her success, yet I was a little bit jealous. I needed to work on that sin.

My junior year I won the school's speaking contest and went on to the district competition. I dreamed of winning that, then going on to the regional and state contests. I wanted to scale the pinnacle of success.

I won the district contest and received a medal for myself and a trophy for my school. Now I was getting somewhere. Leo was proud of me. Lela was proud of me too. She had helped me overcome my speech impediment. But when I learned that the state contest for the humorous division would be held on Sabbath morning, my aspirations drained from me like water through a sieve. I felt it was best not to win the regional contest since I could not participate in the state contest. When my number was called, my body trembled as I walked up on the stage to give my reading. There I stood alone, spotlighted on that huge platform. Among that crowd of people, I knew I was alone on a religious issue too. None of them would understand why contestant number 5 lacked the will to win.

"What happened to you?" Miss Berthoud scolded as she met me at the stage door. "You've never done so poorly!"

"I don't know," I shrugged. But I did know. I wanted to fail so that I would not have to face another Sabbath crises. I won second place and was surprised to get that.

Miss Berthoud was disappointed. "You didn't put yourself into it," she repeated. "You could have won that contest!"

The spring Junior-Senior Banquet was coming up. I wanted to go but feared I would face other conflicts with my religion. There would be a nice dinner, then a dance and a movie. What would I do if one of the boys asked me to dance? And, I couldn't go to the theater either. I never had, and I planned that I never would.

I helped my class make all the arrangements for the banquet, then at the last minute decided that I would risk attending it myself. So Dad and Mom took me to Sioux Falls to purchase my first, store-bought dress. It was a filmy, blue fabric over green satin. As I slipped into my lovely dress that night, I felt like Cinderella headed for the ball.

Most of the juniors and seniors met at the school and rode to Sioux Falls with a faculty member or on the school bus. Hilda, Helen, Annette, and I crawled into the same car, admiring each other's prom dresses.

The banquet room was beautifully decorated in silver and pink. I had drawn roses on the pink menu and dance cards with silver ink. After all the tedious hours of art work, it was rewarding to see the cards decorating every place setting throughout the banquet room.

TESTING TIMES

After dinner, some of the kids danced, but most of them just sat and talked. I stayed in a corner with some lively conversationalists, and we laughed ourselves silly.

Then it was time for the movie. I had planned to sit in the banquet room until the movie was over, but the hotel closed up the room when the other kids left. I was afraid to sit in the car alone in the big city and wondered what I could do. I hadn't anticipated this problem. When my group said, "Come on, Mildred, let's go", I declined. Of course, I had to explain why.

"Oh, well," several said, "if you aren't going, we'll stay with you."

Bless their hearts. They sat in the car with me, and we had a lot of fun just talking. When the evening was over, I was happy. I had had a good time and ended up with a clear conscience.

The week before school was out, the Student Association held the yearly popularity contest. I had received no votes my freshman year, and only the most likely to succeed my sophomore year. I hoped my schoolmates would vote me at least one honor my junior year. When the returns were announced, however, I was overwhelmed. I won most talented, most likely to succeed, most congenial, and best personality. The student body had awarded me first place in over half the categories for girls.

And what about my erstwhile freshmen girl friends who had dumped me because I was too straight? They won nothing. I hadn't needed them to become popular or successful. I earned the respect of my high school friends by simply being what I thought Jesus would have me be. I didn't need to be like the worldlings nor did I need to compromise my principals. God blessed my sincere efforts. My relationship with God was strengthened during those high school years as I passed the tests of faith. For that relationship, and not for the honors, I was gratified.

CHAPTER 4

CAMPING WITH INDIANS AND SAINTS

By 1939 everyone in the family except Julius and I had left home. Nels lived on a farm near us; Dorothy worked as a nanny for a rich family in California; Jean was in western South Dakota; Martena moved to Oregon; Lela taught school at Redfield, South Dakota. Even Gladys, my closest sibling, was out in Washington, D.C., completing her two-year college degree. I knew the time was rapidly approaching when I too would be expected to leave the nest. I wasn't anxious for that time to come; I loved the security I felt at home. While I wanted status-quo, I couldn't impede the changes that time brings. No longer was my family closely entwined as we had been when I was a child.

I was thankful that Lela would be home the summer of my junior year. We were similar in disposition—creative, mischievous, vibrant, optimistic, and spiritually inclined. We enjoyed each other's sense of humor.

The first night Lela was home, we laid elaborate plans to make the most out of the last summer we would spend together. For me the most thrilling event listed on our agenda was the trip we would make to the Black Hills in western South Dakota as junior camp counselors. I had never been more than 100 miles from home and the prospects of this journey filled me with anticipation. I did not have long to wait— it was our first scheduled activity for the summer.

The day introducing me to world travel arrived. Lela and I, bags and bedding in tow, met our transportation at an assembling point. I had imagined that we would be traveling in a streamlined motor coach. What I saw waiting for us at the crossroads more closely resembled a motorized covered wagon! It was an old stock truck with canvass stretched from one slatted side to the other for a roof and bales of prickly straw shoved against the sides for upholstered seats. I sidled up to Lela, "I can't believe this, Sister Thompson! That make-shift cattle cart is eons from first class."

"Try fifth—if class goes that low!" Lela chortled, staring agape at the nameless omnibus. Soon Lela brightened. "Midge, if the kids can take it, so can we. We're rugged. I hope someone has cleaned out the ah, how shall I say this delicately? Animal droppings?"

"Lela! Stop being gross! Now you've stimulated my imagination and I'll probably smell things the whole 400 plus miles to the Black Hills — even if they've scrubbed it out good with Lysol. Which they haven't," I added as I sniffed around the truck bed. "To say I'm displeased with the prospect of riding in the back end of a stock truck is putting it mildly!"

"Why, Midge," Lela teased, "where's your pioneer spirit?"

"The spirit I'm struggling with right now is not labeled pioneer."

"But, Midge, we've got rubber cushioning on our wagon wheels and paved roads." Lela thought she was being witty. "The pioneers didn't have that luxury. Aren't you thankful?"

Lela wasn't fooling me one bit. She was as dismayed as I at our mode of transportation. "I'm thankful, very thankful!" I quipped, imitating her pretentious

CAMPING WITH INDIANS AND SAINTS

gratitude. "At least we won't have to worry about Indians like the pioneer..." My comment was interrupted by some wild whoops and hollers coming from the back of the truck.

Apparently I was in for another unpleasant surprise. As we climbed up the kitchen step ladder onto the end gate of the truck bed, the little pale faces already aboard suddenly came to life. Clamoring for our attention, they caught hold of us, emitting more chilling sounds than the Sioux on the war path.

"Oh, help!" I groaned. Even Lela was looking pretty grim now.

The truck jerked away from the curb before we chiefs got the little Indians unglued from us and seated. This was only the beginning! Every 30 miles or so we stopped to pick up more excited pow-wowers, while those already aboard delayed us further by draining the drinking fountains in every hamlet. Naturally, this made more frequent pit stops essential. It seemed that either Lela or I was pounding on the rear window of the truck cab every fifteen minutes, signaling a saturation-point-has-been-reached condition.

The noise of the truck and that of the Indian campers was about equal in volume. Half-way to our destination, the tarpaulin frayed and flipped loose, so we were exposed to the bright Dakota sunshine for the last 200 miles. Our hair got hopelessly tangled, our winter-white skin got seared, and my hearing, I feared, was permanently impaired. But the heavenly hideaway we reached at the end of the day came close to making up for the discomforts of the journey.

I had never seen real mountains before, and the beauty of the Black Hills simply enthralled me. I had never imagined anything so majestic—and I thought I had a good imagination. I didn't want to go into the cabin; I just wanted to stay outside and absorb the grandeur. My restless little charges, however, thought more of their stomachs than the purple peaks tinged with golden beams of the setting sun. As I herded them towards the mess hall, I stumbled along behind them, my eyes fixed on the exquisite beauty. I quoted aloud from David's Psalm: "I will lift up my eyes unto the hills. From whence cometh my help? My help..."

"Our help better be coming from Midge," Lela interrupted impatiently, startling me from my meditation. "So get your eyes off those hills."

Sometimes Lela's practicality interfered with my ethereal reveries. She forced me back to concentrate on the mundane of planet earth—the kids and camp duties.

Once I got into the routine, I enjoyed the camp and the children. The 10 days passed all too quickly. I was sorry to leave the majestic mountains to return to the plains of eastern South Dakota. The trip, however, had opened up the world for me. I wanted to see more of it. All of it. Never again would I believe that South Dakota was the center of the world, and I knew instinctively that I would not end up living on the plains that had been my childhood home. Slowly, imperceptibly, I was breaking with my past and being led on a course that would take me to the ends of this world.

When I got back home, Leo Lellelid phoned me. We chatted frequently, and saw each other after the Wednesday night band concerts. We also had regular dates on Sunday afternoons. We had a close friendship, but not a romantic relationship. It might have been heading in that direction had either of us known how to go about it. Lela, however, nipped puppy love in the bud by her quips. "Oh, Midge," she teased, her words dripping with sarcasm, "Your LITTLE LID is coming up the driveway. Is LITTLE LID taking you for a ride in his shiny car? Does LITTLE LID have a little brain under his little lid?"

I seethed under those taunts. Leo wasn't robust, but he was taller than I—which wasn't saying much. I was only 5 foot 2. Leo hadn't reach manhood yet and was still pampering his six whiskers into multiplying. But Leo was well-groomed and -mannered, intelligent, and quite nice looking for a 16-year-old. Lela, however, with her demeaning jests, caused me to break off my friendship with Leo. I began to see Leo through Lela's indictments of him rather than for the caring, Christian person he was—and for the Lutheran minister and missionary he would become. Leo Lellelid was quite a contrast to my cousin Leo Nelson, but I loved them both.

The next big event for the summer was the Adventist camp meeting at Huron. Lela, Mother, and I attended the full session; Dad and Julius could leave the farm only on Sabbaths.

When we first arrived on the campground, the tentmasters asked for volunteers to sweep out the main buildings. The Andersen brothers and Lela and I offered our services. Since Marsdon and Dick Andersen were from the same church district as ours, we had known them for years, but pushing brooms together got us more intimately acquainted. When we weren't choking on dust, we sang. I never had more fun doing free labor.

Before camp meeting proper began, we tried out for the choir and were accepted. The first night after the meeting, Mars and Dick Andersen and Lela and I stood around the piano and harmonized just for fun. The music director, Mrs. Hohensee, heard us and assumed that we sang together regularly as a mixed quartet. She asked us to sing the special music for the morning meeting. We did, and that became a pattern. The Andersen brothers and Thompson sisters quartet was much in demand that camp meeting. We probably sang more than 20 special numbers for various meetings. Though Mom didn't say much, I think she was secretly pleased with our contribution.

A new song that we learned and sang several tunes was, "'Neath the Old Olive Trees." The words of that song really touched my heart in a special way. I visualized Jesus alone—crying, praying, and struggling with the weight of sin in Gethsemane. The scenario gripped me emotionally. I envisaged the angels, their hearts torn with sympathy, hovering near, wanting to succor their creator. Yet they had to withhold that comfort. I always felt like crying when I sang those words:

'Neath the shade of the night, walked the Savior of light,
In a garden of dew-ladened breeze.

Where no light could be found, Jesus knelt on the ground,
There he prayed, 'neath the old olive trees.

'Neath the old olive trees, 'neath the old olive trees,
Went the Savior alone on His knees.

"Not my will, Thine be done," cried the Father's own son,
As He prayed 'neath the old olive trees.

I had never seen an olive tree nor the Garden of Gethsemane, but my mental picture of Jesus agonizing in the garden was fantastically real. I hung that picture in the innermost sanctum of my mind, and there it has remained. "One night, one Thursday night, I want to kneel and pray 'neath the old olive trees in the Garden of Gethsemane," I said, my voice quivering.

"Wow!" exclaimed Marsdon. "Now if that isn't a mighty aspiration!"

"No, I just have a strong intuition that some day I'll be in Jerusalem and have that chance," I said confidently. "I don't know why."

"Oh, come on, Shorty, you're a million miles from Palestine. You gonna' sprout wings and fly over there?" regaled Dick.

"Who knows what my future may be?" I answered, not to be rebuffed.

"Well, keep me informed!" Dick laughed skeptically.

The last Saturday night of camp meeting, the four of us went out for root beer floats—our way of celebrating our 10 days camping with the Saints. It was a nostalgic farewell to a wonderful time that would never be the same again.

CHAPTER 5

DORM RULES—BAH! HUMBUG!!

While we had been at camp meeting, Mars, Dick, and I all signed up to go to Plainview Academy for our senior year. I wasn't wild about leaving home and my high school friends, but Lela insisted. "Midge, you'll want to participate in all of your senior activities. You know you can't do that in public school. You'll run into worse snags than you did your junior year. Besides, I'll be teaching at Plainview again next year, so we can have lots of fun together—just like old times."

Not so! What she didn't mention were the restrictions placed upon dormitory students, and it never was "just like old times."

Mars, Dick, and I were about the only new kids in the senior class. We were used to the freedom of home and public school, so we chafed under the dorm rules: Lights out at 9:30. (I lit a candle.) No selling candy. (I hid candy bars in a shoe box and carried on an enterprise.) No sitting with the boys in chapel unless related. (Mars told the faculty that we were cousins, so the three of us sat together in the middle section.)

Like a good cousin, I helped the boys get girlfriends, and they helped me get a steady beau, Dale. He was a good friend of the Andersen brothers and soon became very special to me. During morning chapels, Dale started sitting in relations row with only Mars between us. Just being that close satisfied us. Bah! Humbug on those rules!

I thought Dale was the most handsome guy on campus, and imagined that the other girls must envy me. Dale was new at the academy that year too. He was a junior. It seemed I had a penchant for choosing guys a few months younger than I, but if they looked like Dale I didn't care.

That year I roomed with Goldie Weber, a veteran of academy life. She knew all the "do's" and "don't's" and seemed the epitome of submissive obedience. I'm sure the faculty expected that Goldie's impeccable behavior would rub off on mavericks like me.

Perhaps that is why our top floor, corner room was seldom checked for irregularities— such as candles and candy. Though I'm sure my flaunting of the rules made Goldie uncomfortable, she never preached to me or told on me. Goldie was the best ever. I felt lucky to be rooming with this jewel.

Some of the academy rules made good sense, though I wasn't ready to admit it yet, while others made no sense at all to me. One rule I disliked was separate play periods for girls and boys. That meant that we active teenagers got exercise only every other night. Then, on Sabbaths the boys and the girls had to walk in different directions. One Sabbath the boys could walk around a two mile trail, otherwise known as the big block, and the next week the girls had that privilege. We students thought it would have been much better for our health and spirits if we could have had daily exercise together—properly chaperoned, of course. There were other little rules that we thought justified our complaints.

Another forbidden student activity was the writing of notes to sweethearts during the evening study period. The logic for this rule was obvious—it wasted time that should have been devoted to studies. But teenagers

DORM RULES—BAH! HUMBUG!!

aren't always logical, so Dale and I wrote notes. (Puppy love can be so demanding.) Now Goldie herself became our reluctant note carrier. The night watchman also did his part. I don't know if our carriers ever read our notes or not, but since those missives were becoming more amorous as the year progressed, they could have been quite entertaining for anyone with a soap-opera addiction.

Of course, the amour was the very reason the faculty had for keeping the boys and girls apart as much as possible. In a boarding school situation "steadies" develop quickly. Once a girl has had two successive dates with a guy, the other guys back off. When a teenager zeros in on one person of the opposite sex, his/her emotions run high as the hormones explode. This can lead to early, poorly-matched marriages, saddling the couple with disenchanted dreams of what could have been. It may lead to illicit sex which nibbles away at the conscience or ends in an unwanted pregnancy. I knew that some of the kids were tempting fate, but rather than advising them to do differently, I held my peace. I didn't want to run the risk of losing their friendship. I hadn't worried about that in high school. I had stood for the right and been respected for it. Why was I afraid of being a Christian in a Christian school?

Popularity was the reason for my cowardice! I coveted popularity. Even my objections to academy rules stemmed from my desire to belong to the "in" group. I thought I had to be as rebellious as some of them in order to be accepted. I wanted to enjoy the degree of popularity that I had reached in high school. So I complained about the rules and, with my Katzenjammer nature, set about breaking some of them. For instance, on Saturday nights we were to wait in our dormitories until time for the evening's entertainment. But Mars, Dick, their girlfriends, Dale and I regularly sneaked out of our dorms to explore the school farm. Any adult would have been perfectly comfortable going along with us, but it gave us a special thrill to be running free and escaping detection. We would always return to the dorms on time for the evening's activities and march obediently down to the dining room with the other kids.

One reason our Saturday night escapades thrilled us was that we successfully and repeatedly eluded Miss Kitstrander, the dean of women. She must have thought that her job included spying, but she wasn't very proficient at it. She made a better Mother Superior than a Sherlock Holmes.

I finally settled into academy life pretty well, and found myself acquiescing to the rules until time came for Halloween. My parents had downplayed Halloween because it was a pagan holiday. Furthermore, we never went from door to door begging for handouts. We Thompson children agreed with our parents that trick or treating was tacky and mercenary. No one owed us anything unless we worked for it. We liked Halloween because it gave us an excuse for a party—dressing up in costumes, playing games, bobbing for apples, and going on hayrack rides. Consequently, I was expecting the school to have a Halloween party. But no. They didn't even allow us to have a mixed play period that night. So we plotted an insurrection. Mars, Dick, Dale, and I laid plans. We agreed to meet in the shadows of the girls' dorm at 5 A.M. Since the girls dorm would still be locked at that hour, we girls would have to leap the five feet to the ground from the window on the first floor landing. Then the group of us would walk together around the big block and return in time for breakfast. To complete our party we'd eat the penny suckers we had purchased for the occasion.

DORM RULES—BAH! HUMBUG!!

It was innocent enough, but we didn't have faculty permission.

This was part of the challenge/fun. Had we asked, I doubt that permission would have been granted.

We revealed our intentions to only a few of the other students, but then the tel-another network took over. We were surprised at the large number who showed up for this activity—perhaps half of the dorm students.

I was the leader of the girls, I suppose. At least I took the initiative, opened the window, and with Marsdon's encouragement took the first, five-foot leap to the ground. I landed right in a rose bush that some villain had planted directly under the window. I had to smother my scream. I was scratched and torn, but at least I had obliterated the plant. Now the rest of the girls could jump safely onto terra firma without getting riddled by a rose bush. I had its thorns embedded in various places in my body. I got enough sympathy and appreciation from the other kids, however, to make it worth my pain. While the guys gallantly assisted the rest of the girls to the ground, Goldie and another girl took me around the corner to extract the thorns.

When we were all assembled, we walked around the big block in the chill of the early morning, inhaling the fresh country air of a South Dakota November. Watching the sun rise that morning was a refreshing, almost spiritual, experience.

We girls had evacuated the dorm without alerting Miss Kitstrander. When she sounded the wake-up bell, she missed the patter of teen-age feet. She searched the rooms and discovered that half the girls were missing.

About that time we returned from our walk and sat down on the steps of the three-story building that housed everything—classrooms, dormitories, kitchen, dining room, chapel, and elementary school. Miss Kitstrander was pretty steamed. We sang "Tis love that makes us happy. 'Tis love that smooths the way. It doth incline, to make us kind, to students every day."

Admittedly my version was a modification of the original song but at least the lyrics rhymed. I thought that should have pleased an English teacher, but Miss Kitstrander was not impressed. She called the principal. He confiscated our box of penny suckers and gave them to his young son to devour. This upset us because each of us had donated a penny to the sucker fund treat.

Then while breakfast spoiled, the faculty secluded us rebels in the chapel, and met to decide our fate. We had empty stomachs, but we enjoyed singing our favorite songs as Lotus accompanied us at the piano.

The verdict was finally delivered. Since the kids were too loyal to identify the ring leaders, the faculty would not suspend anyone. However, we would go without desserts for a week and have only a short Saturday night recreation period—the girls participating one hour and the boys the next. That was the end of it. It seemed fair enough, and we kids felt that we had scored a victory.

The irony of my situation was that I worked for Miss Kitstrander, grading her English papers and teaching her remedial classes. In spite of our work connection, I never felt close to Miss Kitstrander. This was probably not her fault entirely. Miss Berthoud had been my idol for so long that I couldn't make the switch. Further, Miss Kitstrander was not warm towards me nor inspiring. I adapted to my other teachers better.

Miss Voth was my typing teacher. I couldn't get my speed and accuracy up to earn more than a B in the subject. But she encouraged me to hang in there. I'm glad she did, because typing is a skill I have used all of my life.

DORM RULES—BAH! HUMBUG!!

Mr. Christie was the dear, patient man who tried to teach me physics. I could handle the subject matter, but the experiments fouled me up. Every time I did one, I shocked myself, set something on fire, or otherwise wrought havoc.

One day when it was my turn to perform an experiment, my fellow classmates stood outside of the door and begged, "Please, Mr. Christie, may we be excused from class today. It's Shorty's turn to experiment. You wouldn't want her to annihilate our parents' children, would you?" I laughed with them at my ineptitude. I finally earned (and I mean earned) a B in the class. That along with my B in typing was tantamount to failure to my parents who were used to seeing A's on their children's report cards. But I didn't care. I had done my best, and I was having fun.

Elder Sorensen, my Bible teacher, was a missionary on furlough for just that year. Missionaries still thrilled me, and I thanked God for this good piece of fortune. (Or was it providence?) Not only did this good man make the Bible class interesting, but he also inspired me to serve God and others. One day I went to his room for counsel. "Elder Sorensen, I had this childhood ambition to become a missionary," I confided. "But now that I am older, I realize that I'm not worthy of the calling. Shall I bury my dreams, or is it possible that I might develop into a better person some day?"

"Stop right there!" he smiled, holding up his hand. "None of us is worthy of God's love and the salvation He offers. Giving us eternal life is God's idea. He's the One who made the alternate plan to save earth's people. I'm not 'good enough' to save, but God wants to do it. The law can't save me. My goodness can't save me. Only Jesus can. He makes up for my inadequacies and cover my sins with His righteousness. True religion is so simple that it's hard for us to believe that we don't have to do something to earn our salvation. So, Mildred, just accept Jesus, study His Word, pray, and follow the guidance of the Holy Spirit. A relationship with God is a personal matter. I can't convert anyone."

"Wh-what?" I gasped, shocked at this admission. "B-but you're a missionary! Surely you have... "

"No, I never converted anyone. Oh, I presented the message and baptized people, but the Holy Spirit converted them."

"Ah, yes. I understand," I said, relaxing back into my chair. I was relieved that God used missionaries for something.

"Now, Mildred," Mr. Sorensen continued. "I want you to hang onto your goal of becoming a missionary. You can, and you will."

"I don't know. Lately I've been thinking that after I finish my degree in education, I'll just stay in America and work for the youth here. That's missionary work, isn't it?"

"That's true," Mr. Sorensen conceded, squinting his soft brown eyes. "But almost everyone is willing to serve God in the homeland where personal sacrifices and adjustments are few. For some people, 'home' missionary work is just a cop-out. But not everyone is suited for foreign mission service either. It is very demanding and takes a strong person—physically, emotionally, and spiritually. A missionary must be willing to leave family for six years or more. That's a long time. Sometimes, homesickness becomes almost overwhelming, and you wonder if you can possibly hold out emotionally until furlough time. You risk catching diseases that people in America thought of getting. Overseas, you have to speak a different language and to adjust to a different culture and climate. Not to mention food. It takes time—lots of time—to shop and prepare your food. Further, you can't pamper your palate with foods to which you are accustomed. Sometimes your selection is very limited and you eat the same thing day after day. But, Mildred, you can handle all of this. You have an insatiable curiosity and love for adventure. God will bless you and give you the strength and courage to be a good missionary."

I listened carefully to Elder Sorensen's summation of what it takes to be a missionary. The silence of the room was in stark contrast to the turbulent activity taking place in my mind. My fingers alternately clenched and loosened from the arms of my chair as I considered the implications of mission service. Should I? Could I? I loved the Lord dearly, but how could He use a person such as I? My spirit was willing, but my flesh was sinful, impetuous, fun-loving, and at times rebellious. I believed I had a few good points. I championed honesty, justice, and truth. I detested sacrilege, hypocrisy, and artificially nice people. I knew I could never be anything but straightforward. Yet, in my estimation, I did not measure up to the Youngbergs, Christensens, or Sorensens. I had more of the apostle Peter's characteristics.

Inhaling deeply, I rose from my chair, stirred by some mysterious force. "Thank you, Elder Sorensen," I said. "You've inspired me to give mission service serious consideration. I might, I just might, become a missionary."

Then the good elder prayed with me. I left his room a few years more mature spiritually than I had been an hour earlier.

MIDGE ON HER OWN

I survive the dentist's torture chamber. June rewards my courage with flowers and ice cream.

CHAPTER 6

METAMORPHOSIS

About halfway through the academic school year, I got tired of complaining and hearing complaints. Right was right, and I would defend it. To be at peace with my conscience was preferable to popularity. Some of the school rules seemed a bit pharisaical, but the longer I was at the academy the more sense they made. Candles could set the dorms on fire, threatening lives. Candy wasn't good for one's health. Writing notes was a waste of time; not many of the courting couples would ever get married anyway. The younger students who were away from home for the first time hadn't developed enough common sense to make wise decisions. The common sense factor was lacking in most of us older students as well. Therefore, the faculty had to take the initiative and set guidelines. I finally admitted that the school rules were probably more of a barrier against our making stupid moves than a fence limiting our freedom. So I became a defender of the school's rules. A metamorphosis had taken place—I broke loose from my judgmental cocoon and emerged a more responsible, mature person.

One day I was in a room with some students who were griping about the restraints they felt were enforced upon them by the school and the church. "We can't have any fun! No smoking, drinking, movies, dances, or even good music..."

"Wait a minute," I interrupted, becoming rather upset with these kids who had led a sheltered life in Adventist schools. "I'm a member of the Adventist church, and I have lots of fun—more fun than those poor kids who suffer from drunken hangovers, guilty consciences, or fear of pregnancies. I've lived out there on the world's fringes because I had to attend public school. I had a lot more freedom being an Adventist than those kids who were hooked on tobacco, alcohol, gambling, and wild parties. I was my own person and stuck to my standards. I didn't allow myself to become a slave to peer pressure. I was free! A lot of those kids out there in the world envied me; some joined me. We knew what went on in the dance halls—the orgies, the sex, the fights caused from beer-fuzzed brains, the permanent cigarette coughs, the quarrels over card games and gambling.

"Furthermore, what are you calling good music? Some of it's OK. I enjoy a lively beat myself. You and I both know the moods and unholy thoughts created by the suggestive words in some of the songs. A lot of the kids in my public high school didn't go for some of the music you guys think is so great.

"And drinking! We all laugh at the bumfuzzled drunkard who has lost control. But I don't envy his making a fool of himself. Worse yet, what about drunken drivers? Do you know what it is like to attend the funeral of a high school friend who killed himself by driving while drunk? Have you watched his parents agonize?

"Maybe I'm sounding like a goody-two-shoes, but I do defend the church's standards. They are intended not just to keep us in harmony with God but to protect our freedom and happiness. The world is not the Utopia you think it is. It just makes me mad to hear you kids talking like you did. You remind me of the old cow who thinks the grass is greener on the other side of the fence, so she scratches up her neck sticking her head through the barbed wire, and ends up with a mouthful of smart weeds."

I stopped then, knowing I had said enough. No one argued with me; they knew I was dead serious. I hoped that my outburst would help my friends see the world as it really is. I was pleased that some of them did make changes later. I had hoped all of them would, but of course they didn't. This frustrated me. I wanted these Adventist friends to emerge from their cocoons of encapsulated ignorance and fly free. I had a problem accepting that some people, in spite of everything they hear and see, choose to ignore reasonable evidence and statistics. This gave me a microscopic insight into the problem God has with sinners and His infinite patience in trying to save us.

Years later I learned that of the kids in the room with me that day one of the boys became an alcoholic and died young with stomach cancer. A blessed release from church principles? Another boy suffered with emphysema from smoking. What freedom? The standards of the church were too strict, they thought. Too late, they learned that there was a price to pay for the pleasures of this world.

I had just gotten to the place where I could live within the perimeters of the school rules when Dale decided to leave and go home to complete his junior year in public school. I had come to depend upon his friendship so much that I wasn't sure I could survive without him. Outside of Floyd, the boy I had a crush on during my second grade, Dale was the first boy with whom I was really enamored. I cried the day Dale left school. By evening my stomach sympathized with my mind. I couldn't choke down supper, so I left the dining room.

Goldie came up from the kitchen earlier than usual that night. She was wise beyond her years and knew just how to comfort a troubled soul. "Well, Shorty, let's talk about it," she said coming right to the point. "First of all, you will survive this separation. And, contrary to a popular cliche, absence doesn't usually make the heart grow fonder."

"Goldie! How can you talk like that? Love is eternal!"

"Not at our age it isn't," Goldie reasoned. "Every day that passes you will miss Dale less. Eventually you will be dating again."

"Not me. I'm going to be loyal to Dale."

"We'll see," Goldie countered. "Now let's study our physics."

Practical, sensible Goldie was good for emotional, romantic me. I imagined things the way I wanted them while she looked at things the way they were. Dale and I really did miss each other, and the post office benefitted from our separation. I looked forward to his almost-daily letters and spent considerable time composing mine. In the meantime Mars, like a good cousin, made sure I kept having fun.

After Christmas, my cooking class planned a dinner for the faculty. As president of the home economics club, I was primarily responsible for the event. One night after supper, Ma Brown, the matron and home economics teacher, asked me to stay in the kitchen with her to finalize the menu for the banquet. We sat in her office and enjoyed planning a super meal for the teachers. Consequently, I was an hour late in getting to study hall. I carried a note from Ma asking that my tardiness be excused. Miss Kitstrander, the girls' dean, was standing at the monitor's desk thumping her fingers methodically, lightning flashing from her eyes. "Where have you been?" she thundered.

METAMORPHOSIS

I handed her Ma's note. "That is no excuse. You must get permission from me before you do anything like this."

I was stunned. "B-but Ma asked me to stay and plan the menu for the faculty banquet. She said she would excuse..."

"Don't argue with me, young lady. Get to your room now. I shall bring this matter to the faculty tomorrow."

I rushed to my room on the verge of tears. "Goldie, come to my rescue. Miss Kitstrander is going to punish me because I stayed with Ma as she requested. She's so angry she's going to bring it to the faculty—I've been caught between accommodating one teacher and upsetting another. I didn't disobey any rule, did I? What did I do wrong?"

Goldie shook her head. "It beats me. But don't worry. Ma Brown will explain it, and the faculty will understand," Goldie assured me.

Ma did explain it, but the faculty surrendered their responsibility for justice to Miss Kitstrander. They gave her the authority to mete out my punishment for being an hour late to study hall. I paid a high price for their decision—it nearly cost me my faith in man and God.

That weekend Dale came back to the academy to see me. After supper on Sabbath evening, Miss Kitstrander asked me to follow her to the English room. Since I worked for her, I innocently obeyed her, having no inkling of her scheme. When we got there, she locked me in the room alone until ten minutes before the lights were out. I sat in the room and cried angry tears for two hours. The injustice of it all was simply incomprehensible to me. Evidently Ma thought so too, because, when she got wind of my whereabouts, she came up and talked to me through the keyhole.

"Shorty, I'm sorry. I'm the one who should be punished. I never imagined the faculty would let it come to this! Dale is disappointed too. But you come down to the kitchen early tomorrow morning, and you two can talk while I get breakfast."

Bless Ma! She had children of her own, and she understood how youth can be permanently scarred from such an experience. I was scarred deeply. My confidence in "Christian" leaders was destroyed that night; I have had a life-long struggle accepting decisions made by a committee. I view things through a skeptic's eye, asking myself, "Do they have all of the facts? Was this decision made to placate an associate? Was God consulted or were they off on their own?" to defend a principle?"

I had never held a grudge in my whole life. Now I had one against Miss Kitstrander. I was decades in burying it. An offense done to a person when she is young seems more poignant. Perhaps the experience was meant to make me a more sympathetic and understanding person. At least I vowed I would never treat anyone with such cold indifference. There had been times earlier in the year when the faculty, had they discovered my misdemeanors, would have been justified in punishing me. I would not have objected to their discipline then because I honestly deserved it. But being punished for obeying a teacher just never made sense to me.

The next morning when Dale and I met in the kitchen, my eyes were still swollen from crying. Our time together was precious, and we realized once more how much we really cared for one another. Then Dale kissed me goodbye and left. I raced back to my room so no one would see my tears. I flopped down on my bed and stared at the ceiling. I thought, "My life here has become blah: I'm missing Dale; I'm lonesome for my parents; I'm mad at Miss Kitstrander; and I'm disappointed in the faculty.

METAMORPHOSIS

I'd better go home and enroll in high school." I got out my bags and began packing.

Lela got wind of my plans and paid me a visit. "Midge," Lela began, planting herself so firmly on my bed that I knew she had no intentions of leaving until she had made her point. "What happened to you last night was wrong, but we Thompsons are survivors. You need to forgive and forget."

I straightened up and looked her square in the eye. "Lela, IF I can ever forgive, I know I can never forget." I sounded as defiant as I felt.

"Well, that may be good. There is something to be learned from every experience. Maybe when you become a teacher, you'll deal more equitably with your students."

"That I will," I assured her. "Right now you're challenging me to turn the other cheek, but I'm not going to let that woman hurt me again. When I metamorphosed my thinking and began championing dorm rules, I also defended the faculty. Now, some of the kids who have heard about Miss Kitstrander's treatment of me are asking me if I still feel the same way. To tell you the truth, I don't. And if I spread my story around, I can cause a big rebellion. I don't want to upset school life for anyone else, so it is better that I just leave quietly." I paused. "Lela, would you get your foot away from my dresser drawer so I can get my things out of there?" I demanded.

"I'm keeping it shut so you can't. Now you just listen to me."

So I listened. Lela was very persuasive, and I agreed to stay. But things were never the same for me again.

I portrayed a happy, outward countenance, though I lived with inner pain. I had learned to distrust people who represented authority in my church. As my mind questioned their integrity and sincerity, I began to question God. That is scary! As my faith/trust crumbled, so did my inner peace. I hadn't yet discovered a very important truth: my perfect God is NEVER responsible for the decisions made by sinful men. He may try to dissuade them from making wrong choices, but He'll never force them to do His will.

Outside of Goldie, I never discussed the incident with the other kids. I worked for Miss Kitstrander, but we seldom communicated. When I left her room for the day, I put on my happy face and pretended to enjoy the rest of the world. Goldie kept reminding me that God hadn't failed me, and that helped me bring my life back into focus. She even suggested that Miss Kitstrander probably believed she had handled my punishment correctly. I couldn't agree with that idea, but memories of my loving church family back in Colman and my parents' pure religion helped me get back on track.

Within the month I had peace within my soul once more. I pushed the injustice that I felt I had suffered back into the recesses of my brain. I tried not to remember it because brooding over the experience was making me bitter and ruining my disposition and health. Solomon says, "A merry heart does good like a medicine." I knew it was up to me to make that medicine. I encouraged my heart to grow merrier each day by counting my blessings. I still viewed authoritarian figures skeptically, but I wasn't letting that stop me from enjoying life.

Mrs. Liebelt was one of my blessings. She encouraged me to write and produce plays for the Sabbath afternoon youth programs. She got me right back in my element—drama. I wrote "A Lesson In Forgiveness", a play about Abraham Lincoln. It was good for me to do

METAMORPHOSIS

this for two reasons: 1) It gave me a chance to be creative again. 2) It helped me overcome the grudge I held against Miss Kitstrander by writing about forgiveness.

It was quite a job to train Adventist kids to become actors. In high school the drama students knew basic stage performance; at the academy I was training novices. Earl Amundsen, the lead man, played the part of Abraham Lincoln. With makeup, a phony beard, and 1860's apparel, he did a creditable job of the part and made the play a success. I knew then he was destined to become a minister. (Don't the best preachers act out their sermons to some extent?)

I enjoyed our dorm prayer bands, the girls' gossip sessions, senior activities, outings, and new boy friends. For the school picnic, Goldie's mom made us twin dresses with sun bonnets. Together with our dates, we recorded this event on camera just before I fell into a mud hole with water. There was hardly any water anywhere during those days of drought; therefore, I'm still trying to figure out where I found enough water in one place to get wet. At least I didn't tear my dress which was proof of my maturity over my younger days.

In the spring, the choir traveled to Oak Park Academy in Iowa for the music festival. I had never been out of the state before, so this was a new experience for me. This time I rode in an old school bus, which was several classes above our junior camp stock truck conveyance. We were even housed in a nice hotel. At least, I thought it was nice. But I was no connoisseur of hotels either—this being the first one I'd ever stayed in.

I roomed with Goldie. Right next to us was Wilma Brenneise, a cute little German girl. I loved to tease this innocent little sophomore because she could hand it right back.

MIDGE ON HER OWN

Soon after we got unpacked, Wilma came to our room. "You know what?" she asked, her eyes and voice expressing shock. "They gave us towels, but no washcloths."

I had called the desk with the same complaint myself and was informed that the hotel did not furnish washcloths since they were often stolen. On a sudden impulse I decided to play a little joke on Wilma. "Well, what do you know?" I asked in mock concern. "I think I can do something about that for you. I'll just call the desk right now and ask them to give you a washcloth. Now they will probably argue with you and tell you that they don't provide washcloths. But they can make exceptions, I'm sure. I'll bet if you just hang in there, they'll recant and give you one. Be firm, Wilma."

So I pretended to call the desk and talked convincingly into the telephone receiver. "Desk? Yes, the girl in room 222 really wants a wash cloth, (pause) I know you don't usually provide washcloths, but couldn't you do it for just this one person? (pause) Well, would you please talk to the manager? (long pause) He will make an exception this once? Very good. I'll send her right down. Her name is Wilma Brenneise."

I turned to Wilma, smiled triumphantly, and sent her on her way. Then I followed at a discreet distance and hid behind a stairwell. Wilma strode confidently to the desk. "I'm Wilma Brenneise, and I've come for my washcloth, please."

They argued the case with her, but Wilma stood her ground. So did the desk clerk and the manager. At last they persuaded her that she could not get a washcloth. It was then that Wilma realized she had been tricked. She ran up the stairs yelling, "Mildred Thompson, you come here. I'm going to kill you."

I wasn't afraid. There was a hint of humor in her voice. I raced up to the room to join her. We both rolled

METAMORPHOSIS

on the bed convulsed in laughter. That special memory of wonderful, jovial Wilma has remained with me through life.

Soon the busy, last days of school were upon us. It was a time for reflection. My senior year at the academy hadn't been perfect, but it had helped me mature. I had learned to live with dormitory rules and a houseful of kids of varied personalities. I had developed Christian leadership through the youth and Sabbath School programs. I had enjoyed the kids and teachers.

Dale came back to school for the commencement exercises. Many of his friends were graduating seniors. Dale's presence, however, created an awkward situation for me. Goldie's prediction had come true—I was going steady again with another young man. I couldn't face either of them comfortably. Fortunately, my mother, sister Jean and her baby Lois were there so I excused myself to be with them. Thus, I, the coward, avoided spending much time with either young man. Amidst the flurry of graduation activities, I don't think either of the guys even sensed my discomfort.

Just before I left for home, Elder Sorensen came to the car to say goodbye. He grasped my hand. "Congratulations, Mildred, on the completion of the second lap of your education. Now it's off to college to get a degree in education, and then in about six years I'll see your name listed in the Review as a missionary, won't I?"

I looked up into his soft brown eyes which reflected Christian love and goodness. "Yes, Elder Sorensen," I managed to say, my voice trembling, "I still plan to become a missionary, the Lord willing."

I didn't know where or when or how, but the mold was set.

MIDGE ON HER OWN

Sunbathing with the maid next door. Tough work!

CHAPTER 7

ON MY OWN

We drove back home after graduation, and I settled in for the summer. After the first few days of the excitement of being home again had worn off, I was surprised to discover that I actually missed the busy academy life. My only link with my academy days now was Carl. He had taken the place of Dale in my heart, and I looked forward to his letters. I was in love again.

"What are you planning to do, Midge, now that you've graduated?" Mom asked. "I suppose you'll leave home and go off on your own for college or work." There was a touch of sadness in Mom's voice as she spoke.

The truth of the matter was, I really didn't want to be off on my own—not yet. I didn't want to leave the sheltered home nest—not permanently. I had gotten terribly homesick at the academy, and I wasn't anxious to go far from home again. However, since my parents had no money to send me to college, the only logical suggestion came from sister Gladys. She had just graduated with her secretarial degree from Washington Missionary College (now Columbia Union College) and had taken a job in the Kansas Conference office. In a letter she encouraged me to take the job she had just left in Silver Spring, Maryland—being a maid for the Bresner family. I could work part-time and go to school part-time as she had to get her college degree.

Mrs. Bresner even sent me a letter, encouraging me to come and work for them. She said that the work was light, and she would help me go to school. It sounded good, so I accepted the job. I would have preferred to go to Union College because it was closer—only 200 miles from home. Furthermore, Lela had saved some money teaching school so that she could return to Union to finish her degree in education. I wanted to go to Union and room with her, but I didn't have the money for the entrance fee.

My parents encouraged me, "You know we can't help you financially, Midge. But if you want a college education, go for it.

God will help you. We suggest that you take elementary education. There are a lot more openings for that than there are for English teachers." I didn't like that suggestion, but it made sense.

A few weeks later, Lela and I left Sioux Falls on the same day on the same bus. As we rode along, I had to keep dabbing moisture from my eyes. It had been especially hard for me to tell my parents and Julius goodbye. But another separation was just ahead. Though I was 18, I had never lived anywhere without my parents or Lela. When we changed buses in Omaha, I clung to Lela in a final, tearful embrace. Then she boarded her bus south to Lincoln, and I went east to Maryland. I wept at the parting, but I also mourned the passing of the happy times Lela and I had shared as loving sisters. Those days were gone forever.

As our bus rolled past miles of Iowa cornfields, I tried to rid myself of the empty, lonesome feeling. I was afraid of being on my own. I knew, of course, that God was with me, but He didn't talk and laugh with me like Lela. In the bus I cried silently, turning my head toward the window so that I didn't make a spectacle of myself. But a young man noticed me and came over to sit with me. He was friendly enough and helped me forget my loneliness. By evening, he became too friendly. Now that I was on my own, I needed to learn how to handle these situations. Since I really didn't know what to do with him, I confided in the lady across the aisle from me when our bus stopped for a midnight break. She said, "Move over with me, and I'll tell my husband to take your seat."

That did the trick. All through Indiana, Ohio, and Pennsylvania, I had pleasant female companionship and protection. She was amused with my "oohs" and "aahs" as we rode through the beautiful mountains.

Mrs. Bresner met me at the bus depot. She appeared slightly drunk, and she drove that way too. I decided I would not ride with her more than necessary—if we got home safely. Not being worldlywise, I didn't know how to detect an alcoholic. Gladys had recommended Mrs. Bresner; I presumed she hadn't turned to booze in just three months.

I was there only a week when the lady flew into a drunken rage, threw down the white, ruffled curtains I had just ironed, demanding that I wash and iron them again. She yelled at her children and did other obnoxious things. Her behavior was so foreign to anything I had seen that I knew I had to leave. I wished I had the money to go home, but Mrs. Bresner had sent me the money for my bus ticket to Washington; I had to stay with her long enough to work off my obligation.

June and Betty Flatten, dear friends from my Colman Church, were also in Washington seeking their fortunes. I called June and arranged to meet her and Betty in church on Sabbath. I told them my predicament. I wasn't experienced enough to handle this on my own. June suggested that I call the college placement office, have them line up another housekeeping job for me, work off my debt at the Bresners, and then leave them.

MIDGE ON HER OWN

Monday morning, after Mrs. Bresner left to have tea with a friend, I called the college. They had just received a request from a Mrs. Meyers for a housekeeper. So I applied for the job. Mrs. Meyers came over to interview me and hired me on the spot. Her Southern hospitality meshed well with my Midwestern upbringing. We immediately felt comfortable with each other. Of course, Mrs. Bresner flew into an outlandish rage when I gave her my two weeks' notice. She promised me all kinds of benefits if I would stay, but I knew it wouldn't last. So it was a happy day when Mrs. Meyers drove me and my few possessions to her home at 7710 Chicago Avenue, Silver Spring, Maryland. I felt a burden had been lifted from me. Now I could relax and need no longer fear Mrs. Bresner's violent temper.

When I walked into the Meyers home, Dad Arthur, 13-year old Patricia, and 17-year old Arthur Jr., greeted me warmly. Immediately, I became one of the family, not just their live-in maid. My work was easy—I only had to vacuum, polish the silver, put on meals, and send out the laundry. The Meyers hired other people to do the yard work, wash and wax the floors, do the windows, etc. She became my pal and confidante, and he my educator. I learned a lot about architecture from this kind man. I'm not sure just what Mr. Meyers's title was, but he had something to do with building the pentagon. At nights he unrolled huge sheets of blue prints, explained the complexities of the enormous government structure-to-be, and told us that they had to drive down pilings into the marshy land to secure a firm foundation for the building. A few times he drove us, his family, as near as possible to the construction site. (The building proper was not begun until September 1941). Somehow, I felt I had something to do with building the pentagon, and I couldn't even read a blueprint.

ON MY OWN

June worked for a very nice family in Bethesda. She was nanny for their two children. Betty found work at the college itself, so she moved into the dormitory. That left June and me to team up on our days off, Wednesdays, to see the town. On Sabbaths we met at the college church with Betty.

Even though June was the age of my sister Gladys, we were a matched pair. We two country girls from South Dakota were like babes lost in the woods of Washington. I had never seen anything outside of the Black Hills and Oak Park Academy; June's travel exposure was even more limited. Outside of the exciting two-day bus ride

Midge and June at Valley Forge. Washington's winter was tough. Our summer—fine.

from Sioux Falls to Washington, we had seen little of this world. Being poor, I had carried a sack lunch with me on the bus and then supplemented that with a malted milk purchased at one of those fabulous bus depot cafes. I never even suspected that my Greyhound bus wasn't taking me on the scenic route through the towns. Until June and I experienced Washington, I thought large cities consisted of dilapidated high-rises, garbage-littered streets, ragged kids, smokestacks, railroad yards, and traffic with only a few nice houses and parks on the outskirts. Then we two hayseeds, from a town of 428 with one main street, arrived in Utopia. We floundered about the metropolis of thousands, bug-eyed at the palatial homes, monuments, and government buildings. The streets, which ran in all directions, confused us. But we couldn't afford to be confused long—cars and buses bent on flattening pedestrians bore down upon us. The name of the game was SURVIVAL; we quickly learned how to leap across intersections without getting maimed or killed.

We thought Washington was so beautiful and exciting that we enjoyed our confusion. We willingly took any risks to explore its environs. Each Wednesday we rendezvoused down town, ate an inexpensive lunch together, and then investigated some memorial, museum, or government building. It seemed that we would never have enough Wednesdays to complete seeing the tourist attractions. June and I reveled in our culture shock and took to touring like pros. We even attended a session of the House of Representatives. We thought we couldn't beat that for patriotism.

After living in Washington for just a few months, I decided that being on my own was pretty nifty after all. I was having a great time living in the president's city.

CHAPTER 8

LIVING IN THE PRESIDENT'S CITY

Franklin Roosevelt was living in the White House when I arrived in Washington. Dad said that Roosevelt had been living there so long he thought he owned the place or at least could claim squatter's rights. Roosevelt had been elected to an unprecedented third term, much to my father's displeasure. Dad was a straight-ticket Republican and influenced his children to have the same political bias. Roosevelt had brought back booze (Dad blamed him personally) and instituted a public works program which was "costing the tax-payers a bundle." At 18 I didn't share Dad's concerns, but neither did I expect an invitation from the White House.

Even so, being the daughter of a radical Republican didn't keep me from attending Roosevelt's inaugural parade. Mrs. Meyers dropped me off near the parade route. I was supposed to meet June around there somewhere, but so many of the natives were milling about that I canceled that search and headed for the parade. I was too short to see over the crowd, so I politely but indomitably wormed my way forward until I could see the floats and the hoopla. I actually saw Roosevelt himself ride by in an open limousine. Judging from the amount of enthusiasm being generated around me, I decided that I must have gotten on the Democrat's side of the street. It was contagious. I got spirited away with the mass mania, and I yelled and clapped with the others. I later felt a little guilty, clapping for a Democrat, but I excused myself on the grounds that spontaneity was a part of my nature. I didn't reveal that tidbit in my weekly letter home, however. Dad would never know of my disloyalty.

Mrs. Meyers was always doing special things for me. She said I amused her with my curiosity and enthusiasm that never reached saturation point. One day she gave me two tickets to hear Sergei Rachmaninoff play at Constitution Hall. That sounded like a very cultural thing to do, so June and I made plans to attend the concert of this famous Russian pianist. When I looked at the price of the tickets, I knew we couldn't afford not to go. Further, June and I had never seen Constitution Hall, so we would accomplish two goals at one time—absorb culture and view another tourist site.

The evening of the concert, Mrs. Meyers dropped me off at Constitution Hall, and told me to take a taxi home, I finally found June in the lobby. It wasn't easy—the place was swarming with society people elegantly dressed in evening wear. June and I looked at each other, dressed modestly in our church clothes, and laughed. June stated our situation succinctly, "We're just two country bumpkins, huh?"

I nodded and whispered, "June, why didn't you tell me we were to come in evening wear? I would have worn my new pajamas."

We giggled some more but felt very self-conscious. So we concealed ourselves in a dark corner until almost everyone left the lobby. Then we hurried into the auditorium, hoping to find our seats inconspicuously. We had no idea where to go, and ended up needing the help of an usher. As he led us across the auditorium, it seemed that all heads turned and eyes focused on us. He directed us to two empty seats in the middle of a long row. We trampled toes, flushing a deeper pink with every irritated sigh from the people who owned the feet. We had made a grand entrance, which was obviously unpopular with the rest of the crowd.

Rachmaninoff was a fabulous artist, and the whole concert kept me spellbound. The orchestra accompanied Rachmaninoff part of the time, but you couldn't have proved that by me. My eyes were fixed on the guest performer and the conductor. I had their features memorized; I could have picked them out of any crowd.

When the concert was over, June and I decided to wait until the main crowd left. We didn't want to make a grand exit too. Besides we wanted to explore the place—see the flags and emblems of the 48 states placed on the walls of the auditorium.

We were making marvelous progress, and had just found the flag of South Dakota when they turned out the lights. Everyone else had long since left the concert hall, and it never occurred to us that they might close up the place. The auditorium was as dark as a cave; this situation was compounded for me since I am night blind. "Help me out of here, June," I pleaded.

"Over here, Midge," she yelled. "I see a slit of light under a door."

I moved in the direction of June's voice, bumping into seats and damaging my shins. Then I fell down into something.

"Are you coming?" June called impatiently. "And what was that crash?"

"It was I, June. I think I fell into another room. I dismembered a chair or some music stands, I think. Come help extricate me from this mess."

"Oh, for goodness sake, Midge! You didn't get hurt, too, did you?" June sounded more disgusted than concerned. "Just stay where you are, and keep talking so I can find you."

It didn't take June long to find me and pull me out of my predicament. She led me to the door with the shaft of light; we were thankful to find it unlocked. We noted the time—10:48 p.m. It was much later than we thought, so we wanted to get outside immediately to hail a cab. But every door leading to the outside was locked. Now we were frightened! We scared each other even more by imagining our possible predicament. Were we locked in Constitution Hall for the night? Did they open the building only for concerts?

We cruised the hallways in search of a phone. We thought we should notify Meyers or the police. We couldn't find one on the main floor, and we opted not to try the dark, basement area.

Then we discovered an inner door. We had no idea where it led or where we were, but desperation had set in. Breathlessly we opened the door and walked cautiously into the room. We were disappointed not to find a phone or a person. Then off to the left we saw another door. We rushed in that direction but stopped short of opening it. We thought we heard voices on the other side.

"Do we dare?" June asked anxiously.

"Maybe it's our only hope," I sighed, feeling much like a trapped animal. We turned the knob slowly, opened the door quietly, and tiptoed halfway across the room before we discovered the two men sitting at a low table, sipping something from glasses. We stopped abruptly as the realization swept over us that the two men were Rachmaninoff and the conductor. We swooned into each other's arms. I'm sure the reason we were able to remain upright was that we were leaning against one another.

If we had been intimidated by the elegantly dressed concert fans, being alone in a room with these two famous men absolutely drained the blood from our extremities and rushed it to the pit of our stomachs. The two men glanced up, obviously startled. Then they stood politely and smiled kindly at us. I'm sure they guessed we were just lost country bumpkins, but they treated us as though we were invited guests. "What can we do for you young ladies?" the conductor asked solicitously.

A myriad of thoughts raced through my brain, but my mouth wouldn't function. I knew we were definitely where we did not belong, but I couldn't think of a decorous way to extract myself from the predicament. Now I knew how Queen Esther felt going before the king without an invitation. But Esther willed herself into the situation; I did not. Esther had a speech prepared; I did not.

"I, ah, we, aaaah, wh-what can they do for us, Midge?" June stuttered, giving me a punch in the ribs.

"Ouch. Oh, well, ah, yes, ah, we, we would like the artist's autograph," I blurted out. I had no idea why that came to my mind, but for the moment that seemed like a reasonable excuse for our intrusion. "June," I whispered through clenched teeth, "give me a program, anything, for him to write on. QUICK!"

June produced a program from somewhere without ever taking her bulging eyes off the men. With shaky hands I transferred the paper to Rachmaninoff. He signed his name with a flourish, smiled, bowed slightly, and handed the paper back to me. I didn't know whether I should genuflect, kiss his hand, or what protocol was proper under such circumstances. So, country bumpkin that I was, I reverted to my Midwestern culture—I thanked him genuinely as I shook his hand. Aah! That hand! Suddenly I realized that I had touched his magical, musical hand—at least the right one. I vowed I would never wash mine again.

What could we do next? I was flushed out of ideas. I looked to June. She was still staring agape at the men. She never blinked nor spoke. Obviously no scathingly brilliant ideas were hatching in her head. The conductor carried on some small talk, asking where we were from, and I answered him—I think. But I suspected we weren't fooling those men for a minute. So I cleared my throat and tried the forth-right approach.

"Sirs," I said, "we are lost. We've never been here before, and after that marvelous concert we stayed too long exploring the concert hall. Now the doors are locked, and we can't get out." I was surprised how good the honest confession was for my soul. My tongue was loosed at last.

"I doubt that the doors are actually locked from the inside, but they may have been hard to open. However, I would say it is good that you didn't walk out on the street alone at night. It isn't really that safe for young ladies. Allow me to call a cab for you," the conductor volunteered.

"Oh, would you? Two cabs, please," I interjected. "We live in different places."

Then that dear, sweet conductor called two cabs for June and me. He didn't make us feel inferior to him. He treated us with all the courtesy he would have given important people. While we waited for the cabs, the men chit-chatted with us. When the taxis arrived, we thanked the men profusely, hopped in the cabs and rode home in a daze. What an amazing four hours!

I learned a lesson that night that has never been erased from my memory: Genuinely famous people are comfortable to be around. They don't put on airs or act superior. They are great because they are humble.

Two years later, Rachmaninoff died, and I mourned his passing. Our encounter had been brief but impressive. I vowed to treat everyone with the same degree of kindness and respect as I had been treated by the pianist and the conductor.

Mrs. Meyers was pacing the floor when I got home. "Goodness, chile," she exclaimed in her Southern drawl, "Whay y'all been? It's nigh unta midnight, and t'aint safe foa gawls to be out this late alone. Don't ya neva do that agin. This town's full of crim'nals an' pimps, jes waitin' to snatch the likes o' y'all fo white slaves."

She had to explain to me about pimps and white slaves; they weren't in my Dakota lexicon. Her explanation was so graphic that my goose bumps had goose bumps. I resolved never to be out late or alone, ever!

Living in Washington was wonderful, but I soon discovered that big city life had its drawbacks. I had to lock doors, watch out for pimps and purse snatchers and cabbies who tried to cheat me. I also was warned not to accept rides with strangers.

I got this advice none too soon. The next Sabbath I was walking the two miles to church along Philadelphia Avenue—alone as usual. A man followed me in his car, stopped, and offered to take me wherever I was going. I refused, as Mrs. Meyers had advised me. When he became persistent, my alarm switched on. Fear gripped me. Not knowing what else to do, I snapped, "I live here!" Then I raced for the nearest house. As I rang the doorbell, I prayed, "Oh, Lord, please save me. Help someone to be home. And please forgive me for my fabrication."

Evidently I had convinced the man. Before I reached the door, he drove off. I walked on to the college church then, a shaken girl.

June was waiting for me in foyer. When she heard my story she advised, "Take a taxi from now on; it's better to be poor than dead."

DEAD! What a wild suggestion!! But when I read Sunday's headlines, I concluded that June was probably right. A girl, walking in the same area where I had been, was seen getting into a car with a man. He evidently raped and killed her, then threw her body by Sligo Creek. Of course, I had no way of knowing if it was the same man that had followed me, but the thought crossed my mind. That experience pegged itself on the walls of my memory. I still get nervous when I think a person or car is following me.

June and I ate Sabbath dinners in the cafeteria with Betty. That way we got acquainted with some of the college students. We joined a literature band that went to a town in Virginia on Sabbath afternoons. In order to cover our territory in an hour, we each took a separate area. This was an unsafe policy, as I was soon to discover.

I took my regular route that Sabbath afternoon. I knocked at the doors, handed out papers, and chatted briefly with the people as usual. No one was home in the aging house set back in a wooded area at the end of the block. So I left my paper and started to leave. Suddenly, I heard a gunshot and screaming. As I stood on the porch, frozen in my tracks, I saw a man with a double-barrel shotgun fire again at two women running down the road. The one lady slumped. At the same instant, her companion slipped her arm around her and half dragged, half carried her along. My blood congealed, and my heart nearly stopped. I needed to hide. Even though the leaves had fallen, I squatted behind a bush, believing that it might provide a little cover.

From behind my bush I watched breathlessly as the man caught up with the women and beat the injured one with the butt of the gun. Evidently he was out of ammunition or decided to finish her off as cheaply as possible. Blood streamed down the victim's head and back. When she collapsed to the ground, he rushed at the other lady. She screamed and fled down the street. Then he returned to his prey, kicked her body, and rolled her over.

It seemed like eons before I heard the police siren. Evidently someone had heard the commotion and called for help. The man fled on foot among the houses. Not until the police caught him did I feel safe. I feared that the murderer would eliminate me as a witness to his crime—if he had seen me.

The ambulance came, covered the lifeless body with a sheet, and rolled her onto a stretcher. Then I unfolded my body, left my bush, circled around behind the house, and ran back to where my group's car was parked. No one was there so I just leaned against the car until Fred Toale, the driver, showed up.

"What's the matter, Mildred? Are you sick?" Fred exclaimed as he scrutinized me. "You're ashen!"

"No, well, yes, maybe..." I stuttered, reliving the nightmare. Then, feeling secure in the presence of Fred and with my adrenalin gone, my legs turned to jelly. Fred eased me into the car before I passed out.

Fred tried to pry my secret from me. When the others arrived, they grilled me too. But I couldn't bring myself to divulge my story. I wanted to block the horrifying scene from my mind. Telling the others about the murder I had seen would be to relive it. I sat mutely all the way home, knowing that my companions were questioning my sanity. Fred let June off at her bus stop; then he parked at Meyers and walked me to the door.

Later that night June called me, but I was still in shock and wouldn't talk about my experience. I thought I could erase the whole scene from my mind. But that night I tossed fitfully on my bed, seeing reruns of the murder. The next day the story hit the front page of the newspaper. "You were out that way yesterday, weren't you, Mildred? Did you hear anything about it?" Mrs. Meyers asked. My pent-up emotions broke, and I sobbed out the whole sordid story.

Mrs. Meyers put her arms around my trembling shoulders and held me close. "Don't tell anyone that you saw it," she advised. Her voice was even and soothing. "The papers say it was a domestic quarrel. The man was angry, got drunk, and killed his wife. It was her sister that tried to help her escape. They are asking for witnesses, but don't go forward. You won't want to testify in court. It will just shake you up all over again. So let's keep the secret."

Mr. Meyers concurred with his wife's advice. But I could not clear the scene from my mind. At night in my tortured dreams, I heard screams and gun shots and saw the bleeding victim slump to the ground. I probably could have used counseling, but in those days people just worked through their problems alone.

That experience squelched my zeal for literature distribution. I never went back to that town again. I finally told June all about it, and she felt I should have come forward as a witness. But June was a forthright Dakota girl who knew as little of the big city ways as I did. So I never contacted the authorities. The man was convicted of murder without my testimony. The victim's sister was the only witness the court needed.

By now, I realized that there was a greater difference between the president's city and the New Jerusalem than I had at first believed. The wickedness that abounded veiled the luster of Washington—the monuments no longer looked pearly, and the domes didn't reflect gold. Washington was a long way from being heaven.

As we passed through the winter months, the murder scene dimmed from my mind. I had seldom before been depressed for even a short period of time, but that horrifying experience very nearly caused me to lose the ability to cover the unpleasant with happy thoughts. Chats with June, frequent letters from Carl, and weekly epistles from Mom healed my troubled soul. Once more my spirits were soaring.

Then, one day in February, I got a "Dear Midge" letter from Carl. That depressed me. I was in the slough of despondency, and I thought I could never be happy again. It was my first experience of rejection and it hurt badly, even though Carl made good sense—"we're young, hundreds of miles apart, and our loyalties are keeping us from broadening our social life. I've started dating another girl; you should date too."

I was already going places with other guys, but I wouldn't allow myself to call them dates. So I wept over Carl's rejection of me and grieved over my eternal loss of love. There would never be another, I thought. It had seemed OK when I had done the rejecting. But when Carl did it, my ego was punctured, and my spirits drooped like fir branches laden with snow. Mrs. Meyers and June came to my rescue. They reasoned away my cold burden—"There are other fish in the pond." They bandaged my wounds—"you're cute." They inflated my ego—"You've got personality." And I lived again. It was still true; I couldn't be depressed for very long.

Within a few weeks Peter, a junior theology major, became a regular visitor. He was six years my senior and a self-made person. He not only paid his own college tuition, but also had a bank account and a nice car. He took me many places, and we had fun; but I really wasn't ready for another full-time relationship. Besides, I had already allowed myself to get caught up in a curious, anonymous friendship. It had developed so innocently, so spontaneously, that I could hardly noticed it evolving.

During the winter, I had become friends with Virgie, the girl across the street. She belonged to a Protestant church I had never heard of. I was anxious to evangelize her, and she was equally anxious to share her faith. Virgie proved to be more cunning. She used a Balaam plot. One night when I visited her, she talked about her pastor's handsome, 22-year-old son, trying to arouse my interest, "I don't need men," I opined. "I think I'm done with them."

But she called Al, told him she had a friend she wanted him to meet, and handed the telephone to me. Now the history of my life reveals my tendency to leap for the here and now and accept the consequences later. I leaped. I talked to Al. He was an engaging conversationalist and intrigued me no end. I became his mystery friend. I wasn't willing to give him my name or phone number, and I talked to him only when I was at Virgie's. He urged me to reveal myself, but I hesitated. There was something tantalizing about this incognito relationship even though my psyche told me it wasn't very smart.

Al told me he played the trombone in his church's band. If I ever came to his church, that was a way I could identify him. (Hmm! A church band would have been a heretical addition to my church's services.)

Finally I decided I wanted to see the man whose melodious voice had captivated my curiosity; however, I didn't want to meet him—not yet. Gradually my religious experience was eroding, and my goal to become a missionary was fading. But I refused to recognize the danger signals, I was too caught up with the novelty of big city life and the attention I was getting from men. Perhaps this is what happened to Lot's family in Sodom, but I refused to parallel myself with them. I knew I should guard against being unequally yoked with someone other than my faith. But my Katzenjammer Kid nature wanted to explore the forbidden, then hope to jump free before the finish line.

One night I deliberately put myself in temptation's way and went with Virgie to her church. As we entered the sanctuary, the band was playing some jazzy music. (Sometime later I recognized it as a corruption of hymns with syncopation and many additional flourishes.) My eyes searched for the trombone player. Aah! What a guy!! I stopped and stared at him for a few moments. He had blond curly hair and a perfect physique and was more handsome than I had imagined. His winsome personality came sparkling through, even when he played his horn. My heart fluttered into double time.

"That's him," Virgie whispered, lifting a finger in his direction.

"I know," I gulped, pushing her hand down. I dragged her behind a pillar in the church where I could sneak a peak at Al occasionally, but I made sure he didn't have the same advantage. If he saw me with Virgie, he would suspect that I was the mystery girl.

Then the band played "The Lily of the Valley" with so much zip and swing I felt like dancing in the aisle. Other folks did a lot of two-stepping before they slid into their pews. I stayed in my seat and complimented myself on my self-control. After all, I was in a church—or was I? The next few hymns were played with the same syncopation and foot-stomping beat. WOW! My church was never like this! People began clapping and singing, and so did I. This was a party in a pew! Some mysterious force seemed to move me unconsciously out of my reasonable self. I was gliding blissfully along in a current of emotional swells.

How subtly the devil works to steer us from the truth! I thought I was strong spiritually. I was the girl who stood up to my high school principal to keep the beginning hours of the Sabbath; I was the 16-year-old that discussed doctrines with the priest and insisted that he stick to the Bible only. I was the junior who refused to dance and go to the movie at the Junior-Senior Banquet. I had set some of my worldly academy friends straight on what they weren't missing. I was the girl dedicated to mission service. Where had my faith and convictions gone?

I needed to get myself squared away spiritually, but amidst the existing pandemonium that was impossible. Then the minister stood and began the service. His prayer drew "amens," "hallelujahs," "praise the Lords," and some incomprehensible chatter from the congregation. His sermon seemed to generate electricity throughout the crowd as individuals kept flicking on and off, powered by some unseen being. Then the preacher switched from a modulated baritone voice to an eerie tenor falsetto. He engendered the Spirit to fill souls and give them the gift of tongues. My antenna went up, and I prayed in my heart, "Not me, Lord. Don't let that spirit work on me. I don't want the gift of tongues —English suits me fine." My body tensed; I expected the devil to appear physically at any moment.

Suddenly, unexpectedly, a lady behind me let out a shrill shriek. I catapulted from my seat. The next second I found myself draped over the pew in front of me. As I balanced my body, I watched out of the corner of my eye as the lady waltzed, crawled, and rolled down the aisle, muttering and crying. Virgie grabbed my flailing legs and helped me back onto my feet in front of my own pew. I stood transfixed, the hair on my body standing at attention.

"Ah, yes, come, sister," the minister encouraged someone in my area. "Let yourself go, Sister. Be filled with the spirit, and speak in tongues."

Virgie nudged me. "He's talking to you."

"Oh, n-n-no, n-n-not m-m-me," I squeaked.

"Then, sit down," Virgie said firmly, slapping me on the legs.

I folded back into a sitting position, but sat on the edge of my pew, poised for flight. Every time another person screamed and muttered, I went into orbit again. Then the band struck up "When the Saints Go Marching In."

"Oh, yes," cried the preacher in his holy voice. "You saints, come marching down," he paraphrased, and his flock responded. There were probably 130 people down at the altar, each speaking a different gibberish. No one understood anyone, but all were impressively sincere. The preacher laid his hands on their heads, blessed them, and told them they were now saved since they had the gift of tongues.

I personally doubted that the spirit of God could function at all amidst such mass confusion. I looked around me. Virgie was still beside me, and my hair was still saluting. Fortunately, most of the back pews were now empty so I couldn't be startled from aft. But neither could I relax; my body tingled. As I rocked on the edge of my pew, people were still being "filled by the spirit, and receiving the gift of tongues".

A few minutes later, I turned to Virgie, "I want out of here." ' She smiled easily. "Sure. Go out to the foyer and wait for me there."

"Easy enough for her to say," I thought grimly. "Her body isn't filled with lead like mine."

After several attempts, I made it to my feet and stumbled out to the foyer. A little later Virgie came out, and someone took us home.

Virgie and I remained friends, but I never wanted to attend her church nor talk to Al again. Their religion was too emotionally stimulating for my conservative Protestant up-bringing. I'd stick with my tried and true and leave the spirits to them. Virgie's religion seemed to work for her. I would not ridicule her faith, but I knew mine had slipped.

Since God couldn't get my attention any other way, this experience served to alert me to my weakening spiritual condition. I had always had spurts of spiritual growth and moderate times when I just coasted along, but seldom had I known a deteriorating connection with God. If that's what living in the President's City was doing to me, it was not good. But thank God for the promises in Romans 8: Nothing could separate me from the love of God.

CHAPTER 9

COLLEGE? HO! WEDDING? NO!

After my experience in Virgie's church, I took a solid look at my personal relationship with God. I saw where I had become careless in little things, depended too much on my own ingenuity, and drifted into a lukewarm condition. I had been too busy discovering Washington, socializing, and making money to put enough time into my spiritual life. I wanted that to change—now. My ritualistic, weekly Sabbath School and Church attendance and my faithful tithing did not satisfy my desire for a closer walk with Jesus. I knew how to change this. I got down to the basics again—Bible study and prayer. And God drew me right back to Him. Again I felt His presence when I prayed, and I imagined He smiled down on me, just as Mother had pictured Jesus to me as I child. I recalled Mother's words that inspired my soul and lifted me up to Him: "Jesus is happy when you talk to Him, Midge. He smiles at God and says, 'There's our child Midge praying. What can we do for her this time?'"

Although I felt close to God again, I gave up the idea of becoming a missionary. I didn't feel worthy of the work. I didn't know what constituted a calling, and I didn't have the faintest idea how to go about getting the job. So I let my childhood dream slip into the furthermost recesses of my mind. If God needed me as a missionary, He'd have to get pretty direct about it. In the meantime, I decided the best plan was to prepare myself spiritually and educationally for the future.

MIDGE ON HER OWN

I saw a lot of Peter that summer. We went on picnics and Sabbath drives, spent weekends at his home, played miniature golf, and went to the zoo. Usually his sister Cathy, his friend Bill, and June went with us.

One Saturday night the guys asked June and me to go bike-riding at Tidal Basin. I was gung-ho on the idea, even though June tried to dampen my enthusiasm. She pulled me aside and whispered under her breath, "Do you know how to ride a bike?"

"No, of course not. You know we Dakota country kids never had bikes."

"Well?" June suspended her question in the air to clinch her point.

"Well, it can't be that hard," I reasoned, disputing her very logical objection. "Just try it and you'll succeed." (I think those were the famous last words of General Custer just before the Battle of Little Big Horn.)

June didn't say any more, but I could see she was uneasy with the plans. Perhaps terrorized would describe her mental state more succinctly.

When we arrived at the bike rental, the man asked us if we wanted to ride singly or tandem. Now I knew what a bicycle built for two was, but the word tandem threw me. I thought it meant I'd have to balance myself on the handle bars of Peter's bike. I didn't fancy riding on an iron ridge for an hour or more, so I blurted out, "I'd prefer riding singly."

I ignored June's gasp. I liked the idea of having control of my own machine. After all, I'd driven a car since I was 14, and biking couldn't be any harder than that! (Sure General Custer—it can't be that hard. Just try it and you'll succeed.)

The man brought out a girl's bike, lowered the seat to fit my 5-foot-2 stature, and pushed the handle bars at

COLLEGE? HO! WEDDING? NO!

me. I slid onto the seat, gave June a reassuring smile, and pressed on the pedal.

Whoa! The two wheeler wanted to list to one side or the other, t wobbled so badly I knew I would fall. But before I crashed, the bike man yelled, "KEEP PEDALING! PEDAL FASTER!!"

So I pedaled, faster and faster. I didn't want to fall. I had no desire to scalp the grass nor skin my legs. As I sped away from my group, I could hear Peter calling in the distance, "Hey, Midge! Wait for me!"

I wanted to wait, but now that I was launched I didn't dare stop pedaling. I desperately hoped that someone would catch up with me and tell me how to stop the thing without tearing up my flesh and/or the real estate. How I wished I'd taken the time to get a few rudimentary instructions in biking. As I glanced at the water off to the left side of my path, I wished I'd learned how to swim too. I feared I would have to veer off to the left to miss a pedestrian, drop into the Tidal Basin and drown. Riding off the path to the right would be equally hazardous. Since I was night blind, I couldn't see the benches and garbage cans that I knew lurked out there in the darkness. If I hit a tree, I could end up with a concussion. Therefore, I needed to stay on the lighted path.

I was cruising down the pathway at a pretty good clip when two people appeared in the distance. "Lookout!" I yelled. "I can't stop!"

They leaped out of the way just before I clipped off the man's pants cuffs. They muttered some unpleasantries about crazy bikers who thought they owned the path. I wanted to explain my irresponsibility was not intentional, but couldn't turn around to do so. Down the path I flew, steering as close to the middle of the path as possible. I chased more people off the pathway that night than there are pigeons at St. Marks Square in Venice. I was definitely raising havoc with the pedestrians. Then I came upon a couple, lovingly entwined, strolling leisurely along. "Look out for me," I yelled. "I can't stop."

"Of course you can..." Mr. Smartmouth disputed. But there was no arguing with Midge and her runaway bike. At the last possible moment, the man dove for the grass, but he was too late. I caught the heel of his shoe with my front wheel, and stripped it right off. He was just lucky I didn't get his sock too. As he sprawled in the grass, he muttered some fearful speech. I didn't mind his taking my name in vain, but he didn't need to include God. It wasn't His fault. God had been doing His best with me for 18 years—trying to teach me to wait patiently and figure out the results before acting impetuously. God must have thought I descended directly from the apostle Peter, so impulsive was my behavior. But I kept hoping that God would work some transformation in me.

Then I saw a bridge looming up in the distance. Now I had three options: 1) Ride into Tidal Basin and drown. 2) Hit the bridge abutment and get a skull fracture. 3) Turn onto the turf and tear up my body in the grass. I began to pray, "Lord, save me. Next time I'll wait for instructions. I'll learn. I will."

Just as I had to make a choice, Peter raced up. "Stop!" he puffed.

"How?" I screamed.

"Put on your brakes! Pedal backwards."

I reacted immediately. I pedaled backwards so hard, the bike came to a screeching halt, catapulting me off onto the grass. I lay there inert for awhile; Peter bent solicitously over me. I was pleased to discover that I wasn't dead—just bruised and badly shaken.

"Midge, you don't know how to ride a bike!" were Peter's first words. I didn't have to guess how he had

COLLEGE? HO! WEDDING? NO!

figured that out; it was obvious. He even sounded a bit agitated as he announced, "Tonight you'll learn! I'll teach you to ride a bike!"

I protested. "I'll never need to know how to ride a bike. Let's just walk."

"No," Peter insisted, "it's good to know how to ride a bike. Someday you'll be glad you learned. You almost never learn something that you don't use later in life." (Those words were almost prophetic—later in my life I did have to ride a bike to my work.)

That night, under Peter's instruction, I mastered the technique. (General Custer was right; it wasn't that hard. I tried it and succeeded.) The next day I noted wryly that my bruises weren't symmetrical, but they surely were colorful.

Peter, Cathy, Bill, June, and I decided to take a trip West during July. It included stopping in South Dakota to see June's parents and mine; going on west to the Black Hills, Wyoming, Colorado; and returning via Nebraska, Iowa, and the other states I had seen on my bus trip east. We shared expenses and ate inexpensively.

It was wonderful to be back home again after a year's absence. Mom's cooking was just as good as I remembered it. When we got ready to leave, Dad drew me aside and said, "Peter's not for you, Middy. He's a good boy, but you don't love him. It won't work."

We finished our trip—and we had a good time—but Dad's words of warning kept repeating themselves in my mind. He had verbalized what I had felt deep inside of me all along. I liked and respected Peter, but there just was not the chemistry to make it a love-match. So I planned to break up with Peter before school started. I would start college fresh and release him to find someone else during his senior year.

In early August, Mrs. Meyers' mother died. The whole family drove to Atlanta for the funeral, leaving me to house-sit. The Meyers had lots of valuable silver and were afraid someone might break in and steal it if the house was empty. I was a bit apprehensive because I had never stayed alone in a house in my life. But the first two nights went very well, and I lost some of my fears.

On Sabbath Peter took our group to the zoo. We came home about sundown and had worship together in the living room. After prayer, we discussed what we would do for the evening. Since we were all tired, we decided to just chat a little and part early.

"Let me get some snacks for us to eat while we talk," I suggested. This met with hearty approvals. As I arose to make good on my promise, the door bell rang. Peter went to answer it. When the man at the door saw Peter, he fled on foot.

"Well, what do you make of that?" Peter asked, turning to the rest of us. "As soon as the man saw me coming, he ran like a scared rabbit."

"That is strange, indeed," Bill responded, joining Peter at the door. "I wonder what he wanted. Since the grass is wet from that brief shower, we can figure out a few things. First he came from the south, cut across the grass, and stepped onto the sidewalk about half way to the house. See his wet footprints on the walk?"

"Yes, I do," Peter concurred. "And since the house is on the corner, he couldn't have seen my car on the other side when he walked up to the house."

"That's right. So he wasn't expecting to see you when he rang the bell. When you came to the door, Peter, he got scared and ran."

COLLEGE? HO! WEDDING? NO!

The boys were analyzing the situation like two detectives on a criminal case. "Peter, I heard someone fiddling with the locked screen door just a few minutes before he rang the bell," Cathy said, her eyes wide with fright. "The rest of you probably didn't hear it. But I am sitting just around the corner from the door, and I couldn't hear anything else. I was really frightened. I tried to warn you all that someone was trying to break in, but no one saw my motions. Then, just as I as I got my voice, he rang the bell." Cathy had shed new light on the mystery.

"What did he look like, Peter? Where did he go?" Bill prodded.

"I really didn't get a good look at his face. He was dressed in khaki clothing and carried some kind of bag—maybe a gunny sack. He was probably about 5 foot 10, normal build. He ran across the street into the woods."

"The scenario is coming to me now," Bill said, sounding like a professional investigator. "This man knows that Meyers are gone. Their car hasn't been in the garage for several days. He also knows that Meyers have lots of valuable silver which he could conveniently carry away in a sack. He knew Midge was here, but he thought he could easily overpower her and escape with the loot. But when he saw a man here, he got scared and ran."

By this time the blood had drained from us girls' faces, and the boys began looking a little peaked too. We all agreed that Bill had probably analyzed the situation correctly. I was scared stiff! I was a coward by nature, and a genuine threat made me doubly so. I listened as my friends tossed around ideas.

"It's obviously too late to call the police," Peter asserted. "And the man will probably not come back tonight. He may think we've all moved in. He's been scared off."

"I don't know about that," I said doubtfully. "Thieves aren't scared off too easily. When I was a kid back home, chicken thieves came to our farm one night. I awakened when I heard the dog put up a big fuss. But they weren't frightened away by the dog. One held the dog at bay with a long stick, while the other proceeded to fill the gunny sacks with squawking chickens that he pulled off the evergreen tree. I could see it all from my bedroom window, but I was too scared to move or yell. Fortunately my brother Nels awakened, got the double barrel shot gun, and fired right above the evergreen. That got their attention, and they quickly scrapped their plans. They went crashing through the grove of trees, the dog hard on their tail, snatching off souvenirs from their pants. But it wasn't the dog that scared them off—it was the gun. From that experience, I know that thieves can be quite persistent. I don't have either a gun or a dog, nor any assurance that the thief won't return."

"Well, maybe I should just take the rest of the gang home and stay here all night," Peter suggested.

"No, Peter, that wouldn't look right," I protested. "I appreciate the protection your presence would offer, but I think we should try to come up with another solution. Besides you have to go to work very early in the morning—the thief could come after you leave."

"I suppose that's true." Peter paced the floor trying to think of an alternate plan. "I have it. You stay in the dorm with Cathy tonight."

"I couldn't do that," I objected. "Meyers expect me to house-sit here. I promised them, and I couldn't go back on my word."

"Well, that's fine under normal circumstances, but what about this?" Peter reasoned.

COLLEGE? HO! WEDDING? NO!

"I've got it," Bill smiled, pleased with his plans. "Let Cathy stay here tonight with Midge. They can sleep with the telephone right beside them. Then if they hear any noise, call the police."

The look in Cathy's eyes indicated her reluctance to volunteer her services. I wasn't comfortable with the plan, either, but felt I had no choice. When the others left around 10 that evening, I locked all of the doors securely. Then Cathy and I prayed that the angels would surround the house and make themselves appear like armed men—like they had for Elisha at Dothan.

We girls crawled into the twin beds in Meyers' bedroom with the phone on the night stand. I could not relax, however. Every little noise set me on edge. I scolded myself, "Where is your faith, Midge?"

Shortly after midnight, the front door bell rang. It sent a chill of terror through me. For some crazy reason, I got out of bed, crept to the dining room window where I could peek through the Venetian blinds to see who was standing at the door. Somehow, I thought it could possibly be Meyers returning from Atlanta. It wasn't! There, with a bag in his hand, was a man in khaki clothing, about 5 foot 10, medium build. The intruder had returned! I slid to the floor, my whole body trembling with fright. I turned on the radio full blast as I crept past it into the bedroom. My hands shook as I dialed the police; my voice trembled as I gave them our location. They promised they'd be right over.

Then I waited uneasily for the police to answer my call. I could hardly breath as I heard the man cut the screen and unlock the screen door. Then he tried various ways of trying to force the front door open. For a few minutes there was silence. Then I heard the basement door window crash. He was trying to force his way in there, but I had removed the large turn key from the inside key hole, and he couldn't budge it. Silence you could slice reigned for a few minutes. I shook in my bed. In the moonlight, I looked over at Cathy. She lay deathly still; probably she had ceased to breath.

Next the thief tried the kitchen door. I knew that was his easiest access. The door was concealed from the street and the neighbors. He could take his time to work on this one. How I prayed then!! I wanted to crawl under the bed, but found I was frozen stiff like Cathy. Just when I felt that all hope of being rescued was gone, the police car arrived.

I heard the police circle the house from different directions. A shot was fired. In a few minutes an officer called through the door,

"Hello. Police are here. We saw the intruder run across the street and into the woods. My colleague has given him chase, but it's doubtful he will get him. May I come in?"

Oh, could he come in! He could stay all night as far as I was concerned!! In fact, I wished he would. My stiff fingers fumbled with the lock, releasing it at last. I wanted to hug this angel of mercy as I pulled him into the hallway. I was able to restrain myself, however, and give him a description of the thief and his shenanigans around the house that night.

The police officer told me that a number of houses in his precinct had been burglarized for money and silver. The thieves hit only the houses where the owners were away. Then he added, "It does appear as if this burglar is becoming more brazen—attempting to get admitted to the house early in the evening by ringing the door bell. I'm sure that he had staked out the house, knew there was silver here and that the owners were gone. I don't know what he intended to do about you."

COLLEGE? HO! WEDDING? NO!

I gulped. I didn't know either, and I surely hoped I would never have to find out. "What shall I do?" I asked, barely able to keep from crying.

"Well, don't worry, little lady. We will cruise around here every half hour for the rest of the night—and every night until the Meyers return. I'm sure he won't come when the Meyers' car gets back in the garage. Will you call the station when the Meyers get back?"

I promised that I would. His colleague came back from the futile chase, and the two men climbed into their squad car and left.

I went into the bedroom where Cathy lay, still motionless, staring at the ceiling. "I only need to fold her hands, close her eyes, and put her in a coffin," I thought grimly. I knew she was still alive, however, when she groaned and her shivers shook the bed.

I looked at the clock. It would be 25 minutes before the police car returned. Would that crazy thief try to slip in between rounds? Then I remembered that our house was on the border between Silver Spring and Takoma Park. Why not call the Takoma Park police too? So I did. In 10 minutes they were there and heard my story. They too, promised to keep a surveillance on the house for the rest of the night. Now I had police cars cruising the neighborhood every 15 minutes—one from Takoma Park and one from Silver Spring. The thief would have to move very rapidly to get anything accomplished between the 15-minute intervals.

I explained the situation to Cathy, and she began breathing again. Then I dropped off to sleep, exhausted from my harrowing vigil.

The next night Peter moved me to the college dormitory to sleep with Cathy. I needed absolutely no prodding—I was most anxious to do so. The next morning Peter took me back to Meyers, and we found everything intact. Evidently the police surveillance deterred the criminal. Meyers came home that day, and I called the police station to discontinue the guard. Meyers were very concerned when they heard my story and were happy that I had not been hurt.

Summer passed and autumn arrived. I enrolled at Washington Missionary College (now Columbia Union College) as a village student. When the business manager interviewed me, he asked me to return to his office after I had finished registering for classes. Since I had so far to commute without a car and had to work half days, I was only allowed to take half a class load. So in no time I had signed up for my classes and was back in the business office, concerned about the manager's request.

"Miss Thompson," he began in a strictly business manner, "when I was talking to you, I was impressed that you are just the person I want for a job here at the college. You have a friendly, out-going personality. Furthermore, you are good in math. Yes, I have checked your high school grades and find them very acceptable." He cleared his throat, and I wondered what was coming next. "Right now I need a young lady such as yourself to be a cashier in the college store. Roland and Spencer are doing an excellent job of maintaining a fresh produce department and stocking the shelves, but they need help. A girl would be a nice addition. Are you interested in that job?"

It took a minute for me to recover from the sudden suggestion and bring my thoughts into focus. I began to ramble. "Oh, that sounds exciting! But I've never run a cash register. Do you think I could do it? I would much rather live on campus than commute the two miles each day. It would be far more convenient and be a saving in time and money. I would have to give the Meyers a

COLLEGE? HO! WEDDING? NO!

week's notice and find a girl to take my place. But, yes, I am definitely interested."

"Good! You have made a wise choice," he smiled confidently. "I'm glad to see you have a sense of responsibility to Meyers. I have a girl already in mind. You may take a week orienting her to your work at Meyers. I'll expect you at work in the college store next Monday. We'll treat you right."

I left the business office walking on air. My life had taken an unexpected turn for the better. I loved a new challenge and working with customers sounded exciting. I would miss the Meyers because they had become my family, but I knew that if I wanted an education I had to earn it on my own. Any work I could get that would facilitate me in reaching that goal had to be taken.

That evening when I informed Meyers of my new plans, there were tears and hugs shared all around. We had become more attached to one another than we realized. But they wanted me to get an education too, so they wished me God's blessing. I oriented Nancy to the Meyers home for one week, then I kissed them a fond farewell and promised to drop by as often as possible.

Peter moved me with my few possessions into the girls' dormitory. I liked my new dean, and the girls were all very friendly to me. I loved my new job and the camaraderie I shared with Spencer and Roland.

After my first month in the store, our sales had climbed. The business manager gave us another clerk—Melvin. I was still the only girl in the store, and the boys enjoyed teasing me. They were also very good to me. Two months later, the sales even eclipsed the first time period. The business manager called me into his office and said that he had decided to give me a bonus for my effort in building up the business. I don't know what he told Roland, but I'm sure he got the same break. He deserved it more than I.

The year was zipping along. I was making good money, doing well enough in my school work, and had a nice room mate. There was just one nagging problem: I still had not made the break with Peter, though I knew I should. I liked him but I felt no real love. The boys at the store encouraged me, "Break it off, Mildred. You just aren't suited." But when I tried, Peter became the more possessive. I thought I would smother.

World War II broke out in December with the Japanese attack on Pearl Harbor. It was surprising how rapidly the war affected the American economy. With boys leaving for the army, there were no young men left to make grocery deliveries to homes. Girls left maid service for the better pay they could get working in factories. Thus a lot of society matrons who were accustomed to having maid service and delivery boys found themselves cleaning and shopping. Diamond-and-fur-bedecked ladies appeared in our college store. They were at a loss to know how to find items they wanted. Self service and shopping carts had not yet become a part of Americana. I pitied these frustrated ladies who were used to phoning in their grocery orders. So when they appeared, I welcomed and seated them, gave them a fresh roll or doughnut—Stan and Fred made the best in the college bakery—took their grocery list, and collected the items myself or asked one of the other clerks to do it. Those rich people became our regular customers because we served them cheerfully. Our business flourished, and we had to add more clerks. I was happy because my bonus check amounted to at least half as much as my hourly paycheck. I not only was paying my school bills with ease, but was drawing out money to buy cloths and whatever else I needed. I even built up a sizable credit.

COLLEGE? HO! WEDDING? NO!

Working 45 hours a week in the college store was fun, but it crimped my study time. I especially needed more time for freshman composition. I loved to write, but being perpetually tired stifled my creativity. We had to turn in a theme every Monday morning, and I had difficulty getting my compositions in on time.

My worst snag came when I had to turn in a typed research paper. I didn't have a typewriter, but my roommate arranged for me to have access to one. She worked in an office on the attic floor of the administration building. She suggested that she leave her door unlocked so that I could sneak up there after I finished work on Sunday night and type my paper. Since I worked 10 hours every Sunday, I never got into the dormitory before lights were out anyway. So no one would notice my absence from the dorm.

That night, Melvin sneaked me into the ad building, and I crept up the squeaky stairs to the top floor with my notes and paper in hand. I found the room with the typewriter, turned on the lights and commenced to type my research paper. I was so tired that my typing was worse than usual. My constant erasing and adding footnotes consumed much time. I became so sleepy that I could scarcely think. About 2 a.m. I dropped my head on the typewriter and fell asleep, slouched in my chair. Several hours later I was awakened by the night watchman. I was so afraid I would be in big trouble that I begged him not to tell the dean. He sympathized with me as he escorted me back to the dorm. He too had to miss out on sleep and work many hours to make his school expenses.

He unlocked the door of my dorm and let me in. I ambled to my room and slumped onto my bed, completely exhausted. The next thing I knew the dean of women was at my door. It was morning, but I was still in zombie land.

"Miss Thompson," she began, placing a gentle hand on my shoulder, "I'm so sorry that you have to work so hard. The night watchman had to report you to me, but we aren't going to worry about last night. I want you to know, however, that if you ever again need a typewriter so desperately, please let me know. I will personally arrange for one to be left for your use in the parlor. It is too dangerous for you to be shut up alone in the ad building at nights. In case of fire, it would be difficult for you to get out. Now get some rest. I'll be around if you need me."

I could have kissed this wonderful lady. After my experience at the academy with the dean, I had not expected such sympathetic understanding.

The English teacher was not as compassionate. He docked me quite a bit for my late paper. It was, I believe, also poorly written, though he was kind enough not to press that point. I had exerted more energy than I had to complete it. I finally got a B in a subject I had always aced, but even that was probably more than I deserved. I felt it was very fair.

Besides a heavy work schedule and my emotional trauma with Peter, I had health problems that year. I never skipped work or classes, but it was a struggle to keep going with the numerous throat infections and low-grade temperatures that plagued me during the winter. Finally the school doctor said that I would have to get my tonsils out. I quickly agreed to the surgery. Since I was 18, I could sign my own papers. I planned that I would notify my parents after it was all over.

I went into surgery on Friday morning, fully confident that I could be back to work on Sunday or Monday. I knew that tonsillectomies were simple procedures. In

COLLEGE? HO! WEDDING? NO!

my case, it didn't turn out that way. In the first place, they gave me too much anesthetic, and it nearly did me in. I wasn't fully conscious until Sabbath morning. After 24 hours I awoke with the doctor sitting beside my bed, trying to force me to drink some kind of stimulant. June and Peter were there too, and they stayed with me on Sabbath. By Monday I was released from sick bay to go to the dorm, but I dressed and went to classes. I was still spitting blood the next week. The infection was so deeply embedded that my throat took a long time in healing.

When I began feeling better, I knew I needed to tackle the breaking-up-with-Peter problem. That school year I had always been too exhausted physically to handle myself emotionally. In a weaker moment, I had even let Peter talk me into getting engaged. How that happened I'm not exactly sure. At the time, I was attempting to explain to Peter there was just no chemistry between us. He told me it was because I was too young to recognize it. He assured me that as we grew older our love would grow stronger and that we would have the perfect marriage. He contended that my father's objection to him was linked to his farmer's syndrome. Then Peter showered me with beautiful, expensive gifts and flowers. He even bought a 12-piece setting of sterling silver for my hope chest. Each gift made it more difficult to break with Peter. It just didn't seem right for me not to appreciate his thoughtfulness. Yet, as spring approached, I began to dread being with Peter. I found it more and more difficult to convince myself that I cared for him.

Although I began feeling on top of the world physically, I was miserable emotionally. I couldn't even sleep well. One night as I was tossing on my bed, I decided to let God settle the problem for me. Out of bed and on my knees, I prayed, "Dear Lord, You know how discontented I am. It isn't fair to Peter either. Please help me to fall in love with him, or in Christian kindness have the courage to break it off. Thanks so much for Your help. Amen."

It was such a relief to push my burden onto Jesus that I fell asleep immediately. Then I dreamed. I saw myself in the mission field, holding a one-year-old daughter, and kissing a man with black hair goodbye. It seemed he was leaving our apartment on mission business. When I awoke the next morning, I felt the dream was an answer to my prayer. It meant I should break up with Peter. He had light brown, curly hair and was not the man in my dream. I know many people would say that the dream was just chance, and perhaps it was. But I believed it was from God. And though I hadn't thought about mission service in months, that was an equally significant point in my dream. Was this God's way of nudging me into foreign mission service?

In the mail that same day came a letter from Carl. He wanted to start corresponding again. He was in college and had broken off with the girl he had been dating. He remembered the good times we had always shared, and wanted to renew our love. Suddenly it dawned on me—Carl had straight, black hair. Was he the man in my dream? The timing of the dream and Carl's letter were uncanny.

I told Peter about Carl, but he would not accept the fact that it was over between us. When he got tears in his eyes, I recanted. I hated myself for being such a coward. "You've got to get nasty," fellow store workers advised. But I believed there should be some Christian way of breaking off a relationship.

In the meantime, with Peter's knowledge, I was corresponding with Carl. We picked up right where we left off, only more serious and mature.

COLLEGE? HO! WEDDING? NO!

The last days of school were upon me, and I was frantically busy—too busy to devote any time to my social life. Besides finishing my class work and sewing my bridesmaid's dress for Gwen's wedding, I made arrangements to have a month off from work so that I could make a trip back to South Dakota. Our family was planning a reunion, and the thoughts of seeing my loved ones again kept me on a constant high. To top all thrills, Lela was getting married and she asked me to be her bridesmaid. Gladys would come all the way from Oregon to sing for her wedding. Feverishly my anticipation grew as I purchased my bus ticket and deposited my steamer trunk full of Peter's gifts at June's house. I tried to get Peter to take back all of his gifts, but he refused, believing I would change my mind.

My last night in Washington was spent at Gwen's wedding. Peter was there too. Returning from the reception he suggested that we set the date for our wedding. I worked up my courage and replied very firmly, "No. Never! I will not set a wedding date because I've told you it will never take place."

I thought that would settled the matter forever, but it did not.

CHAPTER 10

MAKING MAJOR CHANGES

"Bye," I called cheerily to Peter and June as my bus pulled out of the station in Washington, D.C. My exuberance was not reflected in their faces, however. They both had tears in their eyes as they watched my bus turn the corner and head out of town for the Pennsylvania Turnpike. I too, sensed it was the end of that period in my life. But mourning for days gone by had never been my nature. With an optimism born of God, I could always see colorful rainbows in my future. I loved life and eagerly anticipated the next phase of it.

As my bus retraced the road I had taken just two years earlier, I realized how much my scope of the world and my knowledge about life had expanded in that brief period of time. I had lost my provincialism in the sights and sound of the big city; I had rubbed shoulders with the work force and succeeded; I had begun college. No longer was I the scared, naive country girl. (Well, maybe still a bit naive.)

As my bus pulled into the Sioux Falls depot, I grabbed my things and hurried up the aisle. I burst through the open bus door and landed in the arms of my parents and Lela and Gladys. It seemed we couldn't talk fast enough to get caught up on each others' news as we rode home.

We didn't pull into the driveway of my childhood home, however. While I was gone, my parents and Julius became property owners again. They bought my cousin Leo's farm just down the road from our old farm.

It seemed that place belonged to my family anyway, since it was the land where my father and his parents had spent their first year in America in a dug-out sod house. The farm now had nice buildings, newly repaired and painted. Dad had also added a double garage, two chicken houses, a silo, and an entrance and dining room to the house. He had modernized it further with running water and electricity. That was my fix-it, improve-it Dad.

The next few days were a hubbub of excitement. Friends and relatives swarmed all over, and in turn we were invited to their places for meals—so typical of Midwestern hospitality. Then Ramon Cronk, Lela's fiancée, and his parents arrived, sparking more frenzied activity.

On Sunday morning Gladys, Julius, and I decorated the little country church for Lela and Ray's wedding while Mom, Dorathy, and Ethel fixed food for the wedding feast. Toward evening we dressed for the wedding. Lela was a beautiful bride, and Gladys and I agreed that no one was more deserving of happiness than Lela—unless it was us. But happiness, as far as I was concerned, did not involve marriage. I was most thankful to be free of it. Marriage was fine for Lela; she was in love.

The issue of my returning to Maryland for college was often discussed by the family during the days we were together. None of them wanted me to go back East. "Union College is a good school, only 200 miles from home," Julius suggested. "WMC is 1,000 miles farther away than Union. The folks would like to have you closer home, Midge."

"But, I have the best work possible at WMC. I love working in the college store," I argued. "Besides, I get a good monthly bonus."

"There's work at Union College too, and you can come home for holidays." Then Julius looked squarely and suspiciously at me and asked, "Or is it Peter?"

"Oh no," I gasped. "I'm not going back to him. I've already written him my 'Dear Peter' letter. But I suppose if I go back to WMC, he'll try to pressure me to go back to him." The realization struck me suddenly, frightening me.

"That's right. So what about it?" Julius urged.

"I won't make up my mind about college now, so stop crowding me," I said a bit irritated. "I know I won't ever go back to Peter—not just because my family thinks we aren't suited, but because I know I can't live with him."

"That's a good sister," Julius said kindly patting my shoulder. "You know we love you and want what's best for you. These are days of major decisions for you, so I won't even ask about Carl."

"You might as well," I sighed. "All of you know I got a phone call from Carl over the weekend. I told him that I would meet him in Omaha on Tuesday night. Lela and Ray have asked me to ride down to Kansas with them to visit Gladys. We'll stop over night at Cronk's house and Carl will see me there. And I'm not making any promises," I added adamantly.

"Fine!" Julius shrugged his shoulders. "We'll all be praying..."

On Tuesday morning Ray, Lela, and I left for Omaha. When we got there, I showered and dressed for my date with Carl. I chose my clothes carefully. I wanted to look my very best for Carl. I was very anxious to see him after being separated for two years.

At the appointed time, Carl and Mars arrived to pick me up. Carl was as handsome and charming as ever. He gathered me into his arms and kissed me again and again. It seemed natural, comfortable, right. This was perfect love. It had never been so with Peter. We were lost to the world until Mars cleared his throat. "Ahem! I think we'd better meet Dick at the lake, now."

Dick and Mars had arranged to take Carl and me on a boat ride. The setting, I believe, was made as romantic as possible so that I would have little resistance to Carl's initiative. And it was absolutely perfect! The evening sun's rays made golden flecks sparkle on the calm, blue water. White swans swam leisurely about as our row boat glided noiselessly past croppings of water lilies. It was like old times—the Andersen brothers, Carl and I. We had a good time rehearsing our "good old days." Then it was time for Carl and me to be alone for a serious talk. The guys beached the boat, and Carl and I walked over to a secluded area. I didn't want us to make definite decisions on our first meeting, but Carl insisted.

"Midge, I have agonized over our relationship for so long. I can't take it any longer. We must settle the matter, once and for all. Either you go steady with me, or we break off our love affair forever."

Carl made it more difficult for me to make a rational decision by snuggling me in his arms and kissing me. Oh, how I loved him at that moment! I didn't think I could stand the heartbreak of refusing his love. With my head still resting on his shoulder, and emotion tearing at my soul, I said what I knew I had to say, "Carl, I love you so much, but my parents don't want me to marry you. If we go steady again, you know we will get married. Your health problem isn't an issue for me, but it is for my family. Since I will always want their love and approval, I suppose I had better heed their advice. But couldn't we wait—maybe things will change, some new medicine, some..." and I began to cry.

MAKING MAJOR CHANGES

"No, Midge, you'll have to take me as I am." Carl cried too.

We clung together for a few minutes, each feeling the pain of final separation. Without speaking, we walked separately to join Dick and Mars. It was a death walk. We would never tread the path of life together.

Carl went home with Dick, and Mars drove me back to the Cronks. "I'm sorry the evening ended like this, Shorty," Mars sympathized as he opened the car door. "I had hoped for a happy ending."

"So had I," I sobbed, and I ran for the house.

I cried myself to sleep that night. If love gave one so much misery and pain, I didn't want any more of it. The man I didn't want, I couldn't shake; the man I wanted, I couldn't have. I determined to have nothing more to do with men ever! I would become an old-maid like Miss Berthoud—spinster school teachers were the best! My goal was to become a bachelor girl English teacher.

I was not very good company the next day, but Lela and Ray understood. They allowed me to do my grieving as we rode along. The loss of Carl had sapped the life from me. I could hardly lift my spirits out of the doldrums. Then I chanced to notice the setting sun disappearing in a blaze of splendor. The thought came to me that the sun had not died; it was only resting from sight until morning. Just so my life was not over. Happiness had not died forever. I only needed a brief respite. A bright new day would dawn for me again. I could not imagine how soon this would take place...

Before we arrived in Topeka, my spirits were revived. Lela and Ray left me at Gladys' apartment. They drove on to their new home and ministerial work at Emporia.

Gladys and I had supper, then chatted for awhile before retiring. I was super tired and fell asleep almost before I hit the bed. I would forget everything past and think of the future—tomorrow. I still had a lot of life ahead. I'd just wait as patiently as I could for God's surprises.

I don't know if my mid-morning callers were God's surprise or not. Gladys had gone off to work early and left me sleeping. I arose late, ate a leisurely breakfast, and started my shower. Just as I was rinsing the shampoo from my heavy curls, the door bell rang.

"Oh, go away," I said to myself. "I don't want to see anyone today."

But the person at the door continued ringing the bell. "Probably some salesman," I grumbled refusing to answer the door.

Finally, I heard someone call out my name. This aroused my curiosity. I had just arrived in Topeka. Who would know my name and where to find me? I jumped out of the tub, wrapped a towel around my head, and left my body to drip dry as I ran to the door. I shoved the iron turn key in to make sure it covered the key hole.

"Who's there?" I demanded, trying to make myself sound tough.

"Oscar Torkelsen and Wayne Olson," came the answer from the other side of the door. "We just saw your sister Gladys at the conference office, and she told us to come over here to see you. May we come in?"

"Definitely not. I'm not prepared to receive visitors this morning. Besides how do I know you are who you say you are?" Living in Washington had taught me to be cautious.

"We are student colporteurs here in Kansas. You could call your sister to verify that. Gladys asked us to come over here to recruit you as a student for Union College."

"That's nice of you, but I just got out of the tub and my hair is wet," I explained. Under my breath I muttered, "And tell my sister Gladys, alias Miles Standish, to be her own ambassador next time."

"What's that?" Oscar questioned.

I didn't answer. I could hear the other one, Wayne, saying, "Come on, Oscar, let's get out of here. It's obvious she is not going to let us in. This is embarrassing."

Oscar finally became disheartened at my indifference. But like a good colporteur, he pressed for an entrance and a sale. He got neither, so he used the colporteur's last tactic. "All right, Mildred. I'm leaving some literature about Union College outside the door for you. Look it over, and we hope to see you there next fall."

"Thank you. Goodbye," I answered without much enthusiasm.

After the boys left, I dressed and studied the propaganda about Union College. It looked fine to me. My sisters Lela and Jean had both attended Union. But now I dreaded meeting Wayne Olson and Oscar whatever-his-last-name-was when I got to Union College. After all, I hadn't been very hospitable, but neither did I want to let two strangers see me with my dripping hair. Well, maybe Union was big enough for either them or me to get lost. I hoped I would never hear of those boys again, and I was equally certain they would never want to meet me, either.

When Gladys got home that night, we had a good laugh about my visit from the colporteurs. Then we made serious plans for me to try Union for just one year. The next day I wrote to my family's good friend Harvey Hartman, the college business manager, telling him of my desires to go to Union College and my need for summer work.

MIDGE ON HER OWN

In a few days he called me at Topeka and told me to come right away. He had summer work for me.

That day I wrote a letter to June, asking her to remove all of Peter's gifts from my steamer trunk and send the rest on to me.

Then I kissed Gladys goodbye and with my lone suitcase hopped on a bus for Lincoln, Nebraska.

CHAPTER 11

AT UNION COLLEGE

"Miss Thompson? Mildred Thompson?" a nicely dressed young man called as we passengers disembarked from the bus in Lincoln.

"I am she," I responded.

"Good! Mr. Hartman sent me down here to meet you. I'm Art. Happy to make your acquaintance and introduce you to my school. You'll love Union College."

"Perhaps," I said, not too enthusiastically. I was hoping to simmer down some of his enthusiasm, but I soon realized that was impossible.

"You came from Washington Missionary College? Well, Union is the real missionary school. I think we send out more missionaries than any other college." Art stressed this point. He bragged about his school all the way to College View. I only needed to let out a grunt now and then to keep him going. "And see there?" he said, pointing to the top of the administration building, which he claimed had been there since 1891. "That up there is Union's famous clock tower. It not only keeps the student body and the whole neighborhood aware of the correct time, but it's a symbol for us—time is valuable, time is short, our time should be spent in service. Every year we hang golden cords from a picture of the clock tower to the half of the globe where one of our students has gone as a missionary. Union remembers her own.

Maybe one year they'll hang a golden cord for me. What about you?"

"Oh, well, when I was younger I thought about being a missionary, but right now I've got too many years of education ahead of me to think about it."

"Oh, you'll think about it a lot at Union," Art chortled.

Oh, brother, I thought privately! I hope I won't be constantly hassled by evangelists like you.

We had reached the entrance to the girls' dorm. Thank goodness! I didn't want to talk about mission calls or Union College anymore. "Thanks for coming after me and for taking my suitcase to the dorm."

"My pleasure. Be seeing you around," he said cheerfully and ran down the steps. Miss Rees showed me to my room, and I went right to sleep.

The next morning I awoke feeling lonely and frightened. I wasn't anxious to face the future or even that day. Suddenly I didn't recognize ME—the bumbling extrovert, curious and enthusiastic, interested in everything and everyone. Was this inert person, not anxious to get up and get going in a new place, really ME? Then I realized how much the last few months had drained me emotionally. I hoped this complete change would be good for me, even though I was dreading it.

Miss Rees knocked on the door and entered. "Good morning, Miss Thompson," she said formally. "You should go see Mr. Hartman and get a meal ticket and work assignment. And by the way, here's a letter that came for you." She laid the letter down on the dresser and walked out.

She didn't seem very cordial, I observed, or perhaps it was my drooping spirits that made her seem that way to me. I picked up the letter she left, hoping it would be some loving message from my family. When I looked at

AT UNION COLLEGE

the return address, my blood curdled in my veins. It was a letter from Peter. I opened it with trepidation and read the contents. I was shocked at his unkind, hateful words. This was so unlike the Peter I had known. He ended his message by threatening to sue me for breach of promise. This shook me. I didn't know but what he could do that. After all I had promised to marry him. If he took the few hundred dollars of credit I had at WMC, what would I do for my entrance fee at Union? What would happen to my future? My education?

Then pent-up fears gave way to sobs of despair. My whole world was crumbling about me, and I saw no way to dig myself out of the mess. Peter was threatening to sue me. I was still grieving for the lost love of Carl. I had left WMC, where I had a good job, to come to Union, where I would be bottom girl on the work force. I missed my friends out East. The only person I knew here so far was talkative Art. I couldn't confide in him. I needed to counsel with someone; I needed emotional support. But to whom could I turn? Feeling completely frustrated, I cried big, heaving sobs. I didn't think I could ever quit weeping, but I finally did.

I forced myself to shower and dress. I ate the rest of the lunch Gladys had sent with me on the bus. I dabbed powder around my red eyes and went to see Mr. Hartman. He immediately put me at ease. He gave me the good news that my account had already been credited with a few dollars from Lela's account and my credit from WMC. He had a meal ticket ready and had arranged an interview for me with the manager of the bookbindery. Things were looking up already. "Now, is there anything else I can do for you?" he asked with a smile.

I scrutinized his face carefully. Was he someone I could trust? Could he give me some counsel? I needed advice—now. I grasped his offer. "Sir, can a man sue a girl for breach of promise—like, ah, if she breaks an engagement? If he can, he might take away all of the credit I have, and I might not be able to stay here."

Harvey Hartman leaned back in his chair, squinted his eyes, and chewed on the end of his pencil. "What kind of a man would suggest a thing like that?" he asked, obviously incensed. "No, of course not. Not unless you had a written contract that was signed and notarized. Even then, he couldn't win. I surmise this has just happened to you. Well, don't even think about it. Nothing is going to happen. Let me know if he gives you any more flack. And by all means, forget him! You've got a whole new life ahead of you here. We won't let him touch you. Now go to the bookbindery and see what they have for you."

"Oh, thank you very much, Mr. Hartman," I said, barely able to refrain from hugging him. Outside the sky was blue, and the sun shone again. I hurried to the bookbindery, interviewed the manager, and landed the job. After a good lunch in the cafeteria, I went to work and began making new friends. That evening Miss Rees allowed me to select a room, and a girl helped me unpack and get settled. That summer I learned to love and respect Miss Rees as Union's dean of deans.

The work in the bindery was routine and boring—practically no interaction with others. So, I left the bindery for work in the furniture factory. I enjoyed that more, even though I sometimes hit the wrong nail. I still missed my work at the college store in Maryland, but I had to take what Union had to offer.

I never heard from Peter again. My trunk arrived safely, minus his gifts, so I suppose he retrieved his investments. I became my old self again and had lots of fun outside of work. Herbert Hill, a friend of mine from

AT UNION COLLEGE

academy days, and his girl friend Betty, and Chris, a young man I met at Union, started double dating that summer. We went to parks on Sabbath afternoons; during the week we played croquet, miniature golf, badminton, etc. and ate more malts than the guys could afford. (Sometimes we girls insisted upon paying the checks).

I breezed through the summer hardly remembering that I was never going to have anything to do with men again. Whatever did I think I was doing dating Chris? Well, we had agreed that it was a just-for-the-summer relationship; when school started, we would stop seeing each other. But friendships have a way of growing, and at the end of the summer, we discovered that our friendship had gone beyond the good-buddy stage. We stuck to our agreement, however, and ended the relationship.

School was about to begin, and students were arriving in droves. Now all I had to worry about was meeting up with Wayne Olson and Oscar what's-his-name. I almost hoped that neither one had made his colporteur scholarship, and therefore would not attend Union College that fall. Pleasant thought for me—unfortunate for them.

Registration day arrived and we students stood in long, slow-moving lines, waiting for our papers to be processed. I got acquainted with the girl in front of me. Her name was also Mildred Thompson, Irene Mildred Thompson. Her parents were missionaries in South America. I was Alice Mildred Thompson from South Dakota. Now if that didn't give the college business office and laundry a headache - keeping the two Mildred Thompson accounts and laundry straight. Mildred and I were so pre-occupied getting acquainted that I hardly noticed the serious young man in line behind us. During a lull in our conversation, he cleared his throat and interjected, "I'm a sophomore at Union College this year.

What class are you in?" He directed his question specifically to me.

"Since I had to work so many hours last year at WMC, I'm still a freshman. I'll be sophomore second semester," I volunteered.

"Glad to meet a fellow classmate," the handsome young man said, extending a hand. I extended my hand to meet his as he added, "I'm Wayne Olson. What is your name?"

I jerked my hand away. "WAYNE OLSON!" I exclaimed. "Y-you made a scholarship canvassing this summer?"

"No, I didn't. I canvassed only four weeks. Then a young man, whose mother was listening to my canvass, stomped into the room, accused me of flirting with his wife, socked me in the jaw and broke it. I had to quit the colporteur work, get my jaw wired, and live on liquids the rest of the summer."

"Couldn't you sue the man for breaking your jaw and ruining your summer?" I asked, getting so involved in his story that I forgot HE was Wayne Olson.

"No. It was in a depressed area of southeast Kansas. The sheriff said the guy was in trouble or jail half the time. He didn't work, either. I couldn't have gotten a decent settlement from him. So I just chalked it up to experience. I guess I was the only colporteur in North America injured by a client this summer. Not a spectacular record, huh?" He paused. "By the way, I didn't catch your name."

"You don't want to know my name," I thought as I remembered our closed-door meeting in Topeka. But he asked again, so I mumbled, "Mildred Thompson," in the weakest of voices, hoping that he would not hear and be embarrassed to ask again.

AT UNION COLLEGE

"Oh, are you Gladys' sister?" A beam of recognition lighted his face.

I nodded, dropping my eyes to examine the tiles on the floor while flames of embarrassment smoldered about my face and neck.

"I wondered what you might look like. I couldn't tell from the other side of the door," he laughed amicably.

My lame laugh fell short of his joke. I felt I must be developing a fever. I stammered something irrational.

"I remember that day when we went to Gladys' apartment. I didn't want to go without giving you a call first, but Oscar insisted that people liked surprises. Someone got surprised, but it wasn't you," Wayne laughed heartily. "Oscar was rather chagrined when he couldn't convince you to let him in. But I surely didn't blame you any."

"You didn't?" I asked, grateful that he understood. I could tell that Wayne was considerably more amused at the incident than either Oscar or I. I hastened to explain, "I was afraid you would think me terribly rude, but I had just gotten out of the shower, wasn't dressed, and my hair was dripping."

"All very understandable. I'm glad you came to Union. Did our visit help?"

"The truth?" I questioned looking Wayne in the eye for the first time. "Not entirely, though I did read the information you guys left. I came here because it is much closer home than WMC." I didn't mention my desire to escape Peter.

Then, as we moved along the line and into different offices, we parted. "Whew!" I thought, "I'm glad that meeting is over. It wasn't that bad. He's rather an understanding person. I hope Oscar is too."

MIDGE ON HER OWN

Now that school had started, I only worked part time in the furniture factory. I didn't like the work much anymore, and I didn't like having to change my clothes several times a day either.

One day in October, Dr. Hagstotz asked me to remain after history class. I worried about his request. My grades had been good; I hadn't missed any classes. What could be wrong? Though I needed to rush to my Spanish class, I stopped at Dr. Hagstotz's desk to relieve my anxiety.

"Yes, Miss Thompson. I'd like you to try out a new job."

"What might that be?" I asked, my curiosity aroused.

"How would you like writing public relations articles about Union College for the city newspapers? Maybe you'll have to supplement that with a feature story once in awhile. I give you the assignment, you write it up, give your articles to me, and I'll submit them to the Lincoln newspapers. You'll be paid per column inch. That is, of course, if you can write what readers will read. But I think you can do a good job for us. The reason I selected you to try out for this job is because I like the way you answer your essay questions on examinations—clear, concise, factual, but interesting. If you can transfer that ability to writing for the newspapers, you've got it made. You'll be paid well."

I hardly knew what to say. I hadn't written for publication since I wrote the school news articles for the local paper my junior year in high school. But I wasn't under any pressure then—I didn't have to produce articles good enough for pay. The home-spun, down-on-the-farm stuff I wrote then would certainly not satisfy the editors of a big city newspaper. Yet I liked to write, and this would be a blessed change from factory work.

AT UNION COLLEGE

"I'd like to try that job," I replied, businesslike. Inwardly, I was giddy with excitement over this unexpected good fortune.

"Good. See me at one this afternoon for your first assignment."

"But I'm supposed to check in at the..." I started to say.

Dr. Hagstotz waved away my argument. "I've already called the foreman and have arranged for you to try this job for three weeks. If it doesn't work out, you can go back to the furniture factory."

"Oh, thank you, Dr. Hagstotz, for giving me this chance. I'll do my best!" I enthused. I was very thrilled about this opportunity that I hadn't even known existed. It also was an honorable out from the furniture factory.

Each week I got my writing assignments from Dr. Hagstotz, and turned my copy in to him on Thursdays. He sent it to the newspaper office. I was always thankful when I read Sunday's paper and saw that they had published my article with little or no editing. That meant I was doing well. Writing became my permanent job for the rest of the year.

Sometimes the words flowed easily, and I could finish my writing assignment in one short afternoon. In three hours I could earn what it would take me 20 hours to earn at the furniture factory. I still needed more money to keep myself solvent, so Miss Rees gave me the job of carrying trays to the sick students. That, along with cutting and setting hair for some girls in the dormitory, gave me all the spending money I needed. I enjoyed the flexibility of time I had in my writing job. I could write when I wasn't busy with other work—I only had to turn in my copy by Thursday. Now I loved Union College.

This writing job was almost more to my liking than the store work at WMC.

I was glad to get in with the girls. I was an officer in the Girls Club, and did the public relations for them. That year it was the girls turn to have open house. They wanted a skit to announce it to the boys. So I wrote the skit, and also acted in it. When we appeared in the boys dorm for worship, there were the usual whistles and noises that young men make to let the girls know they are noticed. Then we gave our skit, graciously accepted their ovation, and left.

As I was coming out of the dining room the next day, Wayne Olson walked up to me. With no small talk or preparation, he simply announced, "I'd like it very much if I could be your escort for the girls open house,"

I was shocked at his invitation. I had understood that we girls were supposed to write letters of invitation to the boy of our choice to be our guest at our open house. Or was it the other way around? By this time I was so confused it really didn't matter. I didn't know the protocol because I hadn't intended to date anyone. But now that Wayne had made it so easy, I simply answered, "Yes, I'll be happy to go with you."

Dating Wayne couldn't hurt any girl's image. He was active in school functions and respected by our fellow students. This would be a chance for me to become better acquainted with this rather reserved young man.

Wayne gave me a beautiful gardenia corsage—my favorite. We had a nice time together at the open house. He was not as shy as I had thought he'd be. Conversation flowed smoothly. So when he asked me to go with him to the lyceum program the following Saturday night, I accepted his invitation.

AT UNION COLLEGE

During that week Wayne walked me to classes and took me roller skating twice. I enjoyed his friendship but failed to catch his growing interest in me. I thought he was just being gallant.

As we walked to the program Saturday night, I gave him my ticket book. Girls did this so the young man could present the tickets to the usher, and she would be free to take her escort's arm.

The following week Wayne began pursuing me more seriously, but I persuaded myself that he was just being friendly. I was not wanting another love relationship with anyone—even a nice ministerial student like Wayne. But if I wanted to go to the lyceum programs, I had to go with Wayne. He had never returned my book of tickets, and I was embarrassed to ask him for them. I innocently supposed it was an oversight on his part. (Some months later he confessed that it was part of his scheme to keep me dating him.) I really didn't mind too much because if I was going to date anyone, I'd just as soon date Wayne.

That Christmas Union College voted to cooperate with the war effort and not give the students a vacation. Thus, there would be more seats on buses and trains available for servicemen who wanted to go home for the holidays. So we went to school during the Christmas season, believing our sacrifice was small in comparison to that of the young men being shipped overseas. We would get our break in February when public transportation would not be taxed as heavily.

During the holidays the dining room was opened every night for socializing and table games. On Christmas Eve Wayne slipped a small package into my hand. I opened it to find a lovely pen and pencil set. The card read, "Love, Wayne."

"Oh, no!" I thought. "Here I go again! I just want to be friends—not sweethearts!" But I didn't reveal my thoughts. Instead, I thanked Wayne for the gift and made no concerted effort to discourage his amour. I'd worry about that later.

One night Wayne laughingly told me how he had come to ask me for that first date. "The night that you girls announced open house to us some of the guys were in my room having a bull session—discussing the female scene, of course. One of the guys commented that he thought Midge Thompson was okay, and that he planned to date her. I thought to myself, 'Hmm, I think so, too.' So I decided to beat him to the girl. I did, and here we are."

"Yep. Here we are," I thought, "but I don't know where we're going to end up." I was not as amused by his story as Wayne was. I wondered who the other guy might be, but was wise enough not to ask. Knowing my impulsive nature, I was rather proud that I could resist that temptation. "Interesting," I commented, smiling. He seemed satisfied with my response.

The first Wednesday afternoon of January, Wayne asked me to go roller-skating with him. I needed to work on my newspaper article so excused myself. The assignment that week was long, and it had to be done by Thursday noon as usual. As I wrote that afternoon, every word seemed to drop magically into place. I was finished by 3 p.m. Then I slipped over to the ad building and handed Dr. Hagstotz the copy a day early. On the way back to the dorm, I decided to treat myself to a stroll around the campus. Even though it was January, the weather was balmy. On the circuit, I met Gerald, a classmate of ours. He suggested that we go to the malt shop and indulge in some calories. After that, we decided we should go roller-skating to wear them off.

AT UNION COLLEGE

We were having a great time skating. Gerald was teaching me to skate backwards and some other fancy steps when all of a sudden a young man took off skating against the flow of us other skaters. Gerald saw him bearing down directly at us. There was no way to avoid a collision, so Gerald ducked, hoping to cushion me on his chest. But Gerald wasn't quite fast enough. My face smashed right into his forehead with such force that it crushed my nose, pushing it to the left side of my face. We both fell. When Gerald saw the blood and the revolting displacement of my nose, he fainted. The supervisor of the gym, whistled the skaters off the floor and brought out a stretcher for Gerald. I struggled to my hands and

Midge was embarassed by the aluminum cast on her broken nose.

knees, so they did not notice my injury when they placed Gerald on the stretcher and carried him off. I began feeling pain in the area of my nose and felt where it was supposed to be. I panicked when I didn't find my nose in the usual place, so I began searching for it on the floor.

Within minutes the gym director and his helpers returned to care for me. They were shocked when they lifted me to my feet and saw my disfigurement and the blood pouring down my face. The director scooped me up in his arms, hurried me to his car, and rushed me off to the hospital. He was not amused by my complaint, "Go back and get my nose—it's somewhere back on the floor."

As I waited in the emergency room, I was in a great deal of pain. It was, therefore, a relief when they took me into surgery and administered some anesthetic. An hour later I emerged with a newly-set nose, covered with an aluminum cast taped to my bluish cheeks. The skin around my eyes was swollen and turning black. I wasn't a pretty sight.

Back at the dorm, the girls surrounded me with love, washing the blood from my hair and clothes. Miss Rees was also solicitous and did everything she could to make me more comfortable. I truly appreciated the kindness everyone gave me, but in spite of their desire to help, they could not relieve the misery I felt during those first few days. Even the medication I was given did little to ease the pain.

When Wayne heard I had broken my nose while skating, he didn't believe it. I had refused to go skating with him so that I could write my newspaper article. He called the dorm that night and Dorathy Reed, my good friend, assured him it was true. The next day he sent me flowers.

AT UNION COLLEGE

I kept myself secluded for a few days because of my unsightly appearance. But I soon realized this was futile since I had to wear that silly-looking nose cast for three weeks, and I couldn't afford to miss that much school and work. Besides I was bored, so I decided to face the crowd. The faculty and students were most kind—no one stared, no one made nasty remarks. I couldn't concentrate very well, however, and I had a hard time remembering what I should for my semester tests that week. I thought my brains were permanently scrambled and that concerned me. But the doctor assured me that I would be fine, and I was satisfied.

Before World War II began, Dr. Everett Dick organized the Medical Cadet Corps for Seventh-day Adventist young men. This was a program designed to train Adventist youth to serve their country in a non-combatant capacity as medical aids. When the bombing of Pearl Harbor dragged the United States into World War II, the Medical Cadet Corps gained popularity. Wayne joined the Corps even though he was a ministerial student and exempt from the draft. He soon became an officer and looked quite handsome in his uniform. In February, the Cadets had a Valentine's banquet. Wayne invited me. I had just gotten the cast off my nose, though it was still swollen and my face discolored. I didn't look very spiffy—even in my fuchsia formal. I hoped that we could be concealed somewhat in a dark corner. Since Wayne was an officer, we were placed at the head table and photographed again and again. Sometimes one could wish that cameras had never been invented.

Our February vacation arrived. Since Wayne's parents had moved to Oregon, it was too far for him to go home for the 10 days, so I invited him to spend the holidays with me. My parents were happy to see me and get acquainted with the young man whose name appeared frequently in my letters. Wayne had been raised on a wheat farm in western Kansas. He thoroughly enjoyed getting back on a farm and working with my Dad and Julius.

When it was time for us to go back to school, Dad took me aside. "You can bring this one back again, Middy," he whispered. I knew that was Dad's way of saying he was rooting for Wayne.

We got back to school, and Wayne started in on a series of illnesses. First he got the measles, along with a dozen other young men in the dormitory. I was overly busy carrying sick trays to all of them. I hated going up into the boys dormitory with those trays because men have a way of making a girl feel very self-conscious.

The measles epidemic was scarcely finished before the boys started having the mumps. Of course, Wayne got them too. When a guy is on a roll, he might as well complete the categories of childhood diseases. The guys teased Wayne about getting every disease possible so that he could have me wait on him. Wayne responded, "Hey, I'd rather have a private date with Midge than to share her company with a community of chumps like you."

Wayne finally surmounted his physical ailments and got back to school and work. He was just getting into the swing of things again when Oscar Torkelsen, the canvassing partner who had taken him to see me at my sister Gladys' house in Topeka, stopped by his room.

"Wayne," he began slowly, allowing time for the wisdom of Socrates to surface. "Things have not gone well for you this year."

"Physically speaking, that is an understatement. I've never had so many health problems in my life. In the fall I got my fingers chewed up in the fan in the furniture factory, then an onslaught of colds, measles and mumps. You are partly right, Oscar," Wayne agreed, laughing good naturedly. "But socially, this year is the best!"

"Yep! You've had some tough luck, and I don't want to see you have any more," Oscar sighed as he watched Wayne put on his socks.

"Thanks, Oscar, you're a real friend," Wayne said, picking up his shoe.

"So that's why I've come to talk to you. It's time you stop dating Midge."

Wayne dropped his shoe. He couldn't believe the bomb Oscar had just dropped on him. "Wha-a-at? Man, are you CRAZY?"

"No," Oscar answered calmly. "She's going to break your heart. She's friendly and cute. Give her and yourself a chance to date around more. You're only 19, a sophomore, and have plenty of time to look for a wife. My advice: Break up with Midge."

Then Oscar dropped a friendly pat on Wayne's shoulder and left the room.

Wayne slumped in his chair, confused, agitated, disturbed, questioning. What should he do? Did Oscar know something he didn't.

CHAPTER 12

THE END OF THE YEAR

Springtime is beautiful in Nebraska. All nature comes alive again, and the courting process on college campuses escalates. At Union College, further stimulus was provided by the Girls Garden Banquet on May 2. That Sunday we girls spent hours decorating a Maypole, hanging colorful Chinese lanterns—we couldn't use Japanese ones during the war—and setting cozy tables for four.

The campus men, dressed in their finest, met their dates in the lobby and pinned corsages on them. Then arm-in-arm the couples walked through the flowered archway onto the front lawn.

I don't know how many proposals were made that night, but I suspect the romantic setting can be credited for quite a few. If the soft music didn't do the trick, the beautifully sung love songs should have. Perhaps this was Miss Rees' simple way of emptying her dorm each spring.

I had a date with Wayne. We had been dating steady since the middle of November. I don't know how I figured this fit into my resolves for spinsterhood. I certainly was ignoring my plans not to have anything more to do with men. Wayne was becoming very serious while I was blissfully coasting along, enjoying our friendship. Nature itself, if not common sense, should have told me that young people of the opposite sex just don't go on and on forever, seeing each other every day and sharing tender caresses and kisses, without it becoming a love relationship. I was the reason for the word naive.

After dinner, Wayne led me over to the edge of the banquet area. We could hardly find a large tree that wasn't being supported by at least one couple, but we finally did. Then he took me in his arms, kissed me tenderly, and told me how much he loved me. I was still considering that confession when he proposed marriage. I almost stopped breathing. I had not believed it would come to this, so soon! I had just begun to wonder if I loved him. I had thought I'd keep dating him, but I was definitely afraid of another engagement. Now he was talking marriage.   For once, I was speechless. Wayne had taken me off guard.

After a long pause, he whispered, "Well, what are you thinking?"

"I, ah, I don't know what to think. I didn't suspect that you were thinking ah, m-m-marriage," I finally got the word out. "I, ah, I need to have time to consider this."

"All right," he agreed amiably, "but think positively. We have our usual parlor date on Tuesday. Maybe you can have your answer by then." He squeezed me so tight that I considered doing what I felt like—faint.

On Tuesday Wayne and I had our weekly parlor date. He pressed me for an answer, but I begged for more time.

Wayne waited another week while I thought and thought. How I wished that I could see into the future so that I could be positive of making the right decision. I talked the situation over with my best friends, Carol and Dorothy. They brought up reasons, all in Wayne's favor: "Wayne's a real nice guy—diligent yet fun, intelligent but humble. He's a Christian with a purpose, and you love him. If you don't agree to marry him, you'll lose him

THE END OF THE YEAR

to some other lucky girl. You know you can't expect him just to keep dating you forever."

"I know," I sighed, "but, well, I was engaged once, and I knew later it was a mistake. Breaking an engagement can be nasty business. I'm scared."

"Well, do you feel differently about Wayne than you did the other guy?" Dorathy asked pointedly.

"Yes, I do. I think I really love Wayne."

"There's your answer," Carol said. "Love is the reason for marriage."

"Right!" Dorathy chimed in. "So get engaged now and get married next summer like Gordon and me. I'm looking forward to our marriage."

On May 11, Wayne and I had another parlor date. This time I agreed to marry him. Wayne was pleased, and I was relieved that I had at last made up my mind. We set the date for sometime the following summer. Now that I had made this major decision, I became excited about the marriage and started planning for it.

There seemed to be an epidemic of engagements around the school. The guys made wagers with one another as to who would be next. Then the man who became engaged would get thrown into a cold shower by the other guys. Girls have a much more civilized way of passing on their best wishes—squeals and hugs.

Now that we were engaged and looked forward to cooking for our husbands, Dorathy and I decided to prove our culinary skills by making a Friday evening meal for Wayne Olson and Gordon Otter, who was from my Colman Church. The potato salad, choplets, and vegetables were almost up to mother's cooking, but the meringue on the lemon pie shrank appreciably. We slipped off the leathery substance and camouflaged the desert with vanilla ice cream. Gordon and Wayne were so much in love with us that they didn't seem to notice any goofs we made. They probably didn't even know what they had eaten, but they gallantly praised our efforts anyway. Dorathy and I were completely satisfied with our success.

After vespers, Wayne borrowed a friend's car so that we could go to the bus depot to meet my sister Gladys. She was coming in from Topeka for the weekend. On the way into the city, Wayne spoke very little—he seemed cold. I thought, "Here I go again. When I finally love someone my parents approve of and get engaged, then he changes his mind. Why didn't I stick to my earlier resolve—to leave men alone and keep my vow of spinsterhood.

I didn't reveal my suspicions to Wayne, but I began to prepare myself for the inevitable. I knew he would be kind enough not to do it while Gladys was there and ruin my weekend, but he would break off our engagement sometime within the next week.

Gladys arrived on schedule, bubbling with enthusiasm. We kept up a constant barrage of conversation on the way home. Again, Wayne was strangely quiet—although he probably couldn't have wedged in a word anyway. Wayne carried Gladys' suitcase to the dorm, gave me a peck on the cheek, and left with only a "See you in the morning."

"He seems rather dull. Not at all like a newly engaged man," Gladys commented as we walked up the stairs to my room. "I'm not sure about this relationship, Midge. Maybe you'd better rethink this one."

"Maybe so," I admitted. "By nature Wayne isn't super talkative, but I know him well enough to realize something is bothering him. Well, whatever it is, I'll handle it when it comes. Whatever will be will be, you

THE END OF THE YEAR

know. I can't worry about it now. You are here, and we're going to have a nice weekend together."

Gladys and I talked way into the night. The next morning we scurried around to get ready for Sabbath School. Then Wayne called saying that he had an upset stomach; he would not be by to pick me up.

"Oh, no," Gladys laughed. "I'll bet your food made him sick. You never were much good in the kitchen."

"Admittedly I'm not the natural-born cook that you are, Gladys, but don't forget, friend Dorathy helped with the cooking last night. It wasn't just me!"

"Well, then, maybe he is sick of his bargain, already," Gladys said with a touch of sympathy in her voice.

"I know," I sighed. I was beginning to regret getting engaged to Wayne. "Gladys, I wished I would have stuck to my vow to forget men. All they bring is heartache. I don't think this thing called love guarantees 'happiness ever after'. Why do you suppose so many songs are written about LOVE?"

"Probably because so many people try it, so folks relate to it. On the other hand, there probably are as many songs written about unfaithful love and broken hearts. Why is that?"

"I don't know," I groaned. "Probably because it occurs frequently. If that is normal, then I must be super normal. I've had my share of broken loves." Then I quickly changed the subject. "Come on, let's hurry to Sabbath School. We're going to have a good time today! So there, Wayne Olson," I said defiantly as I laid his picture face down on my dresser.

I put my concerns aside and had a good day with Gladys. I refused to be depressed. Life was full of so many good things, and I trusted that the Lord would bring them to pass. So why worry?

Toward evening, I got a telephone call from the male nurse in the boys dormitory. "Midge, I think you should know that Wayne is quite sick. I believe he has acute appendicitis. I am taking him to the hospital now. I'll call you again from there after the doctor has seen him."

About 10 p.m. Union's nurse phoned from the hospital. "The doctor confirmed my suspicions. It was a hot appendix, all right. Wayne had surgery at 8 and is now back in his room. He's still pretty groggy from the ether, but he wants me to be sure to tell you that he loves you."

Gladys put an arm around me. "See, Midge, it wasn't your cooking."

"Yeah, I know. But if one of the meals in which I only had a part, gives him appendicitis, what will he get when he tries to subsist solely on my cooking, huh? I'll kill him within a week."

"No, you won't!" Gladys laughed. "Come on! Cheer up! Let's get to bed now so we can go see my future brother-in-law in the morning."

Wayne was happy to see us the next day, even though he wasn't feeling too perky. He even apologized for getting sick and assured me that it had nothing to do with the meal Dorathy and I had prepared. He also wanted to confirm our love. He pulled me down to him and gave me a long kiss. Didn't that solicit whistles from the male companions in his ward!

Gladys went back to Topeka that afternoon, but before she left, she assured me that Wayne was OK in her book.

The following week the rest of us students took our semester tests while Wayne continued his period of recuperation. (In those days, surgical patients were kept in the hospital for 10 days of complete bed rest.) Then school was out, and the students dispersed in all

THE END OF THE YEAR

directions to their homes, work, or the armed services. I too had to leave for my colporteur assignment in Minnesota.

I had never intended to become a colporteur, but it happened so subtly—sort of crept through the back door of my mind without my realizing I'd left the door open. The previous February, the directors for the literature evangelists swarmed onto the campus with an eye for business. Since Wayne was an officer in the colporteur club, I attended all of the meetings to be with him. With my tendency to become enthusiastic about everything except lynching, I was a prime candidate for drafting. In no time at all I was singing "If Jesus goes with me I'll go anywhere" as lustily as the real colporteurs. Somehow, sometime during that week, Miss Lindsey signed me up to canvass in a county in Minnesota where there was only one Adventist couple.

As I said, I never intended to be a colporteur, but the leaders made it sound so easy and so important that I was swept up with their fervor. I did consider the fact that my father first learned about Adventism from a colporteur, and I was certainly glad that he had. So if I could lead someone else to the truth I loved, I thought that I should do so. My decision to go canvassing was made through prayerful consideration. Once it was made, I waded right into it with my usual gusto for a new experience. I eagerly looked forward to my summer's work. I hoped to win some soul in Minnesota to the Lord and urged other students to join this evangelistic outreach.

I went to Wayne's hospital room to tell him goodbye for the summer. As soon as he could finish his final tests, he too would be headed for his "important work" in Kansas. I leaned over his bed and kissed him goodbye—right in front of his buddies. Then I left for the depot and boarded my bus to Minnesota.

CHAPTER 13

BIKES, BOOKS, BULLS, AND WITCHES

I smiled to myself as I sat on the bus headed for Hector, Minnesota, the home base for my colporteur endeavors for the summer. I found the name "Hector" amusing because it sounded so much like "hectic". I trusted that the name would not be indicative of my success there. I was an eternal optimist.

Miss Lindsey, the lady colporteur director, met me at the bus depot in Hector. She was an enthusiastic matron from Sweden with a delightful accent which I enjoyed imitating. She took me to the home of the Laymans, an Adventist couple in Hector, who agreed to shelter my canvassing partner and me for a few weeks. We would not pay rent, but we would help with the yard and house work on weekends and pay our share of the food bill. Neither the man nor his wife was in good health but their spirit of hospitality was refreshing.

On Tuesday morning Miss Lindsey took the bicycle parts out of the trunk of her car. Bicycles were the only mode of transportation for student colporteurs that summer, and we were thankful that the Minnesota conference had invested in the two-wheelers to loan to us. If we would have had cars—which we didn't—we couldn't have used them because of the gas shortage. World War II was escalating by 1943, and an all-out war effort demanded rationing—tires, gas, sugar, butter, etc.

I admired Miss Lindsey's mechanical skills as I watched her assemble my bike. I tried to learn more about the contraptions, but, unfortunately mechanics was not my forté. When she finished the job and shoved the handle bars at me, I rode off like an old pro—thanks to Peter, who had insisted that I learn to ride a bike that night at Tidal Basin in Washington. Peter was right when he said, "You seldom learn something that you don't use sometime later in life." Now was the time in my life that I needed to ride a bike, and I didn't have to take the time to learn. I could start canvassing immediately.

That afternoon, Miss Lindsey left my partner, Pauline, to learn to ride her bike while she took me into the country and introduced me to the real thing. She drove her car since the government gave extra gasoline coupons to people in her type of work. The general rule was that all student colporteurs had to sell in the country; the cities were reserved for the regular, full-time colporteurs.

The farm houses in that area were between one-half to a mile apart. That meant we girls would only be able to make eight to ten contacts per day. In order to earn a scholarship during the 12-week summer, I figured I had to make an average of five complete sales per day. During the colporteur rally at Union College, the literature evangelists leaders made it sound convincingly easy. Now I was about to test the veracity of their claim.

Swedish people lived on the first farm we visited. Miss Lindsey made a real hit with them. As they rambled away in Swedish I listened intently, smiling when they did, nodding at appropriate intervals, but understanding very little. I had learned my canvass as I rode the bus to Hector; now I was wondering if I should have learned Swedish too. I was relieved when the lady told me that, although most of the county was made up of Swedes and Germans, they spoke English as their first language.

Miss Lindsey made a complete sale at the first house; then we went on to make four more stops and four more sales. By the end of the day, my confidence rested on cloud nine—or somewhere beyond. I could see that selling books was much easier than I had anticipated. Being a positive thinker, what I hadn't considered was that there might be hazards in the job—such as dogs and bulls with schizophrenic dispositions.

The next morning I was raring to go. I packed a change of clothes on one side of my saddle bag and my prospectus, Bible, Colporteur Evangelist book, and order pad on the other side. Then I was off to earn my scholarship. Riding far out into the country as we would be doing all summer, I knew I would have to depend upon the hospitality of the people for food and shelter from Monday morning until I could get back to headquarters on Friday afternoon. But this did not worry me. Our colporteur rally song was "If Jesus goes with me I'll go anywhere." I had never doubted God's eternal presence, though I sometimes marveled at His infinite patience in hanging around with me. Besides, I sincerely felt I was working for the Lord. I believed I was doing the people a service by introducing them to my books. During the war many doctors were drafted into military service; therefore, the country folks could certainly use the MODERN MEDICAL COUNSELOR. Ellen White's books would assuredly bring blessings and inspiration to my customers, while the SIGNS OF THE TIMES magazine would evangelize them. I wholly believed in my work. I might never be a foreign missionary, but I felt I was being one here and now.

On my first day out alone, I settled upon an introduction that almost guaranteed me an entrance. After a brief prayer I read the name of the family on the mailbox before I rode up the driveway. If the name seemed German, I would say "Hello, my name is Mildred Thompson. Mem mutter ist von Hamburg." That was more than most Germans in the area could claim—I was first generation American, while most of them were second generation. If the name was Swedish, I would say that my father was Scandinavian—I didn't specify that he was Danish. In this manner I gained access to every home. Those wonderful people of old country descent were very kind to me. Every noon someone invited me to eat with them. And every evening, someone invited me to spend the night in their home and eat supper and breakfast with them too. I had no physical wants whatsoever that summer. Jesus was indeed with me and answered my prayers by providing my necessities.

On Friday of the first week, I returned to my headquarters in Hector. I was elated—I had made 20 sales in the three days. I hoped that this trend would continue throughout the summer. Pauline was elated too. Though she looked like a casualty of the war, she had finally learned to ride her bike. If she healed sufficiently by Monday, she was going to work her territory north of town.

Two more wonderful work weeks passed. My records showed that I averaged nine calls per day with seven or more sales. Pauline was not enjoying the same degree of success in her area. We discussed the situation and decided that the Swedish people might be more eager to buy books than the predominately German folks in her north-of-town territory. So we thought it only fair to swap territories. Among the German people I gained entrance with "My mother came from Hamburg." I had a great time with the German people who lavished me with good food and feather beds. I still averaged the same number of calls and sales. Pauline still was not enjoying much success. Perhaps she did not have the degree of enthusiasm for her work that I had. I really felt I was working for God and enjoyed every minute of it.

Much as I loved my work, I also looked forward to weekend respites when I could compare notes with Pauline, wash my clothes, enjoy the Sabbath, and read my mail—most of it from Wayne. On Saturday nights after sundown, Pauline and I would wander up town to window shop and treat ourselves to an ice cream cone. One night we noticed a set of real silverware in the hardware store. Things like this were becoming very scarce because of the war. It didn't take much encouragement from Pauline to get me to enter the store and purchase the beautiful silverware set with the delicate rose pattern on the handles. I also purchased the last toaster and waffle iron in the store. As I carried my trophies home, I realized how serious I had become about my marriage to Wayne.

Now that I had depleted Hector of small appliances and silverware and we had finished canvassing that area, Miss Lindsey decided to move us to new territory—Bird Island, 10 miles west. We would miss spending weekends with the Laymans—especially the Sabbaths. We were apprehensive about going to Bird Island because there were no Adventists there; finding a weekend headquarters for us became our subject of prayer. We kissed the Laymans goodbye, loaded up our bikes and suit cases, and headed for the unknown.

In Bird Island, Miss Lindsey took us directly to the bank to set up accounts for the down payments we collected during the week. In this small town, the bank president-manager-accountant was Mr. Martin, assisted only by a teller-secretary. We quickly completed the financial arrangement. As we turned to leave, Miss Lindsey said, "Mr. Martin, these girls have a need for housing. During the week they work in the country, but they need a weekend headquarters. Do you know of anyone in town who would rent the girls a room-just for the weekends?"

"No-o-o," he dragged out his response, rubbing his chin as he mentally checked out the neighborhood. "This is a small town with modest-sized houses. We don't have any requests to rent rooms. Off hand, I can't think of anyone from whom you could rent a room. Unless...Just a minute. Let me make a phone call."

We sat down. If he could find us a room, we would gladly wait a minute—even five or ten. Soon Mr. Martin returned, smiling.

"Well, my wife says that if you want to rent our married daughter's room, you can. Our kids are grown and gone from home so we do have extra space—never thought of renting before, though. Ma won't charge you much, but she doesn't want you doing much cooking. Ma's fussy about her kitchen, but you can store your milk and stuff in the refrigerator. Would that arrangement do you?"

"Yes, yes," we chorused. It wouldn't be that long anyway. We had already completed five weekends with the Laymans. We could eat cereal and sandwiches on the weekends since the country folk fed us so well during the week.

So we moved our few belongings into the Martin home. Before we even got settled, Ma Martin adopted us as her girls. She may not have shared her stove, but she shared all of the food she cooked on it with us. We only refused the pork chops.

I was looking forward to going home in just four more weeks. Things had gone very well for me. I was way ahead of my target in sales. I would easily make my scholarship, but I needed to put in about nine weeks of time in order to get the scholarship benefits offered by the conference. Besides, I really wanted to complete the country territory. There had been some inconveniences in canvassing—having only one change of clothing for the five work days, withering in the heat, getting rained on, or being chased by dogs. But I thought canvassing was a wonderful work. I was doing service for God and man while, at the same time, I was earning a scholarship for school. Surely there could be nothing more satisfying than that.

One sweltering afternoon I was riding my bike between farm homes when suddenly I noticed a cold wind sweep over me. I stopped and looked at the peculiar clouds gathering in the west. The wind stopped, and there was deathly silence—then the sound of a freight train rumbling down upon me. Next I saw a funnel-like cloud touch a field near me. It sucked up bales of hay and dirt. In a flicker I knew it was a tornado. I threw my bike down, dived for the ditch, and crawled into the security of the road's steel culvert. Even as I did so, the tornado swept over me. Then it was silent again.

After awhile, I cautiously crept out of my hiding place and viewed with astonishment the devastation wrecked upon crops and trees in just a few moments of time. I heard later that three cows had been carried some distance by the tornado, then dropped in some trees. Some animals were killed, but there was no loss of human life. One man, along with his tractor, was caught up in the funnel. The tractor was dropped about an eighth of a mile away, and the man came down only a short distance from it. He suffered some broken bones but considered his deliverance miraculous. I couldn't have believed the power packed in wind gone berserk if I had not seen the results. Some farmers showed me where straw had actually been driven into the boards of their farm buildings. I was thankful that I, along with everyone else, had escaped.

A few days after the tornado scare I was peddling happily along singing a favorite song of mine—"Anywhere with Jesus I can safely go." I was so intent with the meaning of the words that I scarcely heard the screech of tires as a car slid to a stop within inches of my bike. Instinctively I peddled faster to get out of the way. A couple of sloppily dressed men jumped out of an old jalopy and ran after me, shouting obscenities in broken English. As I glanced back, I could see that they were itinerant farm workers. I couldn't understand much of what they were saying, but I caught enough to know that I did not want to make their acquaintance.

Since I had put distance between us, the men jumped back into their car, rode up behind me again, and jumped out to grab me. Again I escaped their grasp, but I knew I couldn't keep up that pace for long. It was hard pedaling on the gravel road. My lungs were exploding, and I was gasping for air. I prayed to my Savior for deliverance.

Just as the men were catching up with me the third time, a farm house seemed to appear out of nowhere. It had been there all the time, but in my frenzy it had escaped my notice. I rode into the yard, dropped my bike to the ground, and ran into the house. The men did not follow me. I was so out-of-breath that I could not speak. I gesticulated to the puzzled house wife while she mopped my brow with a cold wash cloth. I thrust my prospectus into her hands, and she studied it while I recovered my breath. She wrote out her own order. I signed it, accepted her down payment, and wrote her a receipt. When I finally recovered sufficiently to tell Mrs. Almsted why I was so panic-stricken, she insisted that I go no further that day. I took her advice and spent the night with them. I even helped her with her chicken chores.

The very next day I had another scare. I had reached a beautiful farm home at the end of a long driveway that skirted a pasture. Being a farm girl myself, I had enjoyed the peaceful pastoral scene—cows with their calves and sheep with their lambs grazing on the sweet, green grass. After I completed my canvass and took the order, I hopped on my bike and started coasting down the lane.

I intended to ride slowly along so I could enjoy the tranquil panorama again. But a critter in the pasture made me suddenly change those plans—it was a white bull along the fence line with a mean look in his eyes. I had had an aversion to white bulls ever since my father's white bull had almost killed a man. Our white bull had to be shot since he'd become too mean to load into the truck bound for the slaughterhouse. I believed meanness to be inherent in white bulls. As I glided past this one, he put his head down, bellowed out threats, and pawed up the real estate to prove he was serious. That spurred me into action. I was off like a bullet, pedaling as fast as I could down the driveway, hitting ruts and praying that the ruts wouldn't rip off my tires. The bull had no such worries—his four hoofs carried him with whirl-wind speed down the fence line after me.

As the bull closed in on me, he rammed into the fence like a bomb. Shivers rippled down my spine, and I prayed that the fence would contain him. It did, but he surely put a crimp in the woven wire. The bull bounced off the fence and back onto his haunches as a thin line of blood trickled down from the cut on his forehead.

Now he was MAD! He shook his head, rose to his feet, and charged after me with a vengeance. His delay had given me time to reach the end of the driveway. Then I turned left onto the main road as my next customer's farm was in that direction. Bad decision! The road bordered the bull's pasture for another quarter of a mile. I knew now that I should have turned to the right and hid in the ditch until the bull got the complaints out of his system. It was too late now to turn around. The bull cut the corner and we were off on another sprint—me spinning my bike wheels up the gravel road and the bull tearing up the turf along his fence line. When he was even with me, he made another attempt to fall the walls of Jericho. The fence groaned and a post snapped, but once more the woven wire contained the bull. (Bless those manufacturers of woven and barbed wire fencing!) The bull's attempt, however, delayed him long enough for me to beat him to the end of his pasture.

When I got over the hill and out of the sight of my foe, I dropped to the side of the road. I gasped short, hot breaths, and my blood pressure soared beyond calculating. As I sat in the grass letting my body and my emotions cool down, I thought about my experiences of the last two weeks—the tornado, the men, and the bull. I had spent five weeks canvassing successfully and peacefully. Then the devil set up three scary situations to discourage me. Of course, he didn't succeed—I was too busy thanking God for His deliverances.

I was glad to get back to headquarters that weekend. Ma and Pa Martin always welcomed us home with hugs. While we showered, Ma washed our clothes. Then the four of sat down to a scrumptious meal served in her formal dining room with linen napkins and all. We shared our week's experiences with them while we ate. My white bull story became their favorite. The Martins respected our Sabbath time, and on Sundays we would go to church with them. This served a duo-purpose—the church service was a blessing to us, and it also helped us meet people we might be canvassing during the week.

After lunch, the Martins packed a picnic supper and took us out to places of historic interest. Martins were wonderful people! God had provided us with the best of weekend headquarters.

One Sunday night I got a phone call from the Educational Secretary of the South Dakota Conference. He wanted me to teach the church school in Sioux Falls, South Dakota, during the next school year.

"But," I argued, "I have already earned more than a full scholarship to attend Union College for the next year. I only have a couple more weeks to go to get in my time."

"Never mind," he said. "Get your scholarship and use it next year. I need a teacher there this year."

"But," I protested, "I have only the basic courses. I haven't had teaching methods courses. I don't know if..."

"I'm not worried about that. The Thompson girls are all born teachers. You will do just fine."

What did he know about the Thompson girls' ability? Sure, Jean and Martena were teachers, but they had not taught for him. He was basing all of his assumptions on one person—Lela. She had earned recognition in the teaching profession, and I didn't want to tarnish her reputation by my novice teaching. But the man refused to hear my arguments, and before I hung up the phone I was committed to teaching a year in Sioux Falls.

Then I called Wayne and told him of this twist of events. Wayne seemed a bit disappointed. "Midge, I had looked forward to spending this year of our engagement together at Union. But if you feel duty bound to teach, maybe some good will come of it. However, I'm warning you, I'll be up there every month to see you."

"Thanks for the warning, dear," I laughed. "You'll be welcome."

The next week I met the only person in the community that treated me rudely. Everyone else had been very cordial, even if they hadn't purchased my books. I had canvassed Mrs. Lane (obviously not a German or Scandinavian name) and was just writing up her order when Mr. Lane came in for lunch.

"What's this?" he questioned gruffly, grabbing the order pad from my hands. I was so shocked that I could hardly stutter out an explanation about my selling health and religious books in the community.

"We don't need your books," he said curtly. "And we don't need you comin' around here peddling your false religious junk and medical quackery."

I was stunned to silence as he continued his diatribe.

At last his wife squeezed in a tiny rebuttal, "But all the neighbors have ordered her books."

"That's their problem if they are duped," he retorted. "I'm not so gullible. This young girl probably doesn't know a thing about medicine or religion. I wonder if she's even heard about God or creation."

With that hot accusation, which almost drew fire from me, he tore up the order, thrust the prospectus back into my hands, and ordered me out of the house. I had conjured up a few choice remarks of my own by then but thought it was the better part of wisdom to leave without expressing them. I was sorry to leave poor Mrs. Lane alone with the wretch, but it was Friday afternoon so I cycled back to Martins.

On Sunday morning, Pauline and I attended church again with the Martins. I sat on the end of the pew by the center aisle. When the offering plate came to our row, I reached up to take it from the hands of the deacon. What a shock I had when my eyes met those of Mr. Lane. He was equally stunned. His face turned brilliant red, he dropped the plate in my lap, and turned away. I recovered the plate before it rolled onto the floor. Plainly the man was unnerved. Before the service was over, Mr. Lane left the church and went out to sit in his car.

As we left the church, we were greeted warmly by many of our clients, but I fixed my eyes on Mr. Lane's car. I was tempted to go over there and inquire about his health, but I denied myself the opportunity to heap a few coals. I had already ruined his Sunday.

This experience was very good for me. It made me think of the judgment day when we will have to come face to face with our deeds—unless, of course, we've already made things right with God and man. It helped me learn that I must be more careful with my words. Like the poem says, "Boys flying kites, draw in the white-winged birds, but you can't do that when you're flying words." Poor Mr. Lane was left chewing on some mighty nasty words.

Before I knew it, the ninth week of my summer had arrived. Since I needed only the time, not the money, I decided to make my last week a time of sharing.

On Tuesday afternoon I stopped at Johnsons' house. They had three lovely daughters about my age, and they insisted that I spend the night with them. After supper Mr. Johnson regaled us with stories from Sweden about trolls, lumberjacks, and ghosts. We were having a great time together when suddenly he got very sober. "Mildred," he said, as a strange, frightened look came over his face, "I must tell you. We've got a witch in our neighborhood. In fact, she lives just a half mile north of us."

"You're joking, of course," I laughed.

"Oh, no! Please, Papa," Ingrid pleaded as her face paled, "don't tell any stories about her tonight. It's just too scary."

"I won't. You know I don't like to think about it either. After all, it was I who saw the ghosts floating around her. I just want to warn Mildred not to go there."

With a curiosity like mine, introducing the subject of a witch begged for more details. But Mr. Johnson was adamant. He shut off the subject like closing a faucet. I wanted to tell him that I was a Christian and didn't believe in ghosts, witches, clairvoyance, or any such things. I sincerely believed that the devil could not perform anything supernatural in the presence of God's followers. My college friends and I had sometimes joked about witchcraft and the silly Ouija boards. I knew it wasn't for real.

I assured Mr. Johnson, "Don't worry, I'll not be going north. I intend to take a few houses to the west and then go back to Bird Island. Thursday I'll deliver my books, and Friday I'll take the bus to my parents' home."

We went to bed then, and the witch was almost forgotten. Just before I dropped off to sleep I did wonder how such a strong Swede like Mr. Johnson could possibly be cowered by his neighbor lady, who he thought was a witch.

Wednesday dawned serenely beautiful. What an ending for my last day of colporteur work! I started west, taking the houses as I went. Then, since the homes seemed to be closer together up north, I decided to take just the houses around the section. I met with exceptional success and was basking in the satisfaction of it. Without thinking about it at all, I had come almost full circle and was a half mile north of Johnsons' place. I pushed my bike up the hill of the last driveway, never remembering that Johnson had warned me that this was the house of the witch. It didn't take long for me to figure it out, however. I noticed that all of the shades on the east side of the house were still pulled. Further, the back door was closed. I knew that was strange because country folks left their doors open in the summer. In fact, few people even had locks for their doors. But I brushed my apprehensions aside and knocked anyway. After a long while, a lady opened the door just a crack saying as she did so, "Just a minute. I knew you were coming but I'm not quite ready for you." Then she shut the door again.

"Well, now my reputation goes before me," I mused to myself. "It's about time—this being my last call on the last day of my Minnesota colporteur adventure." It still had not fully dawned on me that I was at the witch's house.

The door opened again. "Now you may come in," the lady said in a whisper-like, mysterious voice. I tried to get a good look at her face before I entered, but she turned her head aside. I did catch a fleeting glimpse of her eyes—empty, lifeless, wicked.

I suspected where I was now. "Calm down, Midge," I told myself. "Remember there is nothing to this spiritualist stuff—just people letting their imaginations pull tricks on them."

I walked up the four steps into the kitchen. It was dark in there too. I suggested that we pull the shade up to let in more light. "NO!" she said sharply catching my hand as I reached for the string. "We like it dark like this—the spirits and I."

Whoa! Now I knew where I was!! And the lady was already talking about spirits as if they really inhabited her place and ran the show. I needed to get the ball back into my court pronto! So I used a favorite old colporteur ploy and asked for a glass of water. The lady took a glass from the cupboard, and I reached for it.

"NO!" she said firmly. "My daughter will get the water for you from the basement. You may not take it from the sink faucet."

By now I was becoming alarmed. What did the water in the basement have in it anyway? No way was I going to drink that water when, and if, it ever came within my grasp.

As my eyes became accustomed to the darkness, I spotted a picture on the wall of the Virgin Mary with the bleeding heart holding Baby Jesus. I knew this was a typical Catholic picture. "Oh," I exclaimed, trying to make small talk, "I see you are Catholic."

"No, we used to be. But we have something far better now. We have the spirits, and you can have them too if you'll do what I say."

"N-n-no," I faltered. "I, ah, don't want them."

I should have left then, but I had to be the conscientious colporteur and try to make a sale at every house. I made another attempt at sane conversation. "I see you have a nice new stove. Hard to come by during these war years, right?"

"Yes," she agreed. "But the spirits lead you to these things. Last month when I was canning, my daughter came to visit me and walked across it, commenting how happy she was that I had such a nice stove."

"Y-y-your daughter walked on the hot stove?" I questioned incredulously.

"Yes," she answered nonchalantly. "She is a spirit too, now that she is dead. She comes to visit us every year on the day she was killed."

I was aghast. I couldn't even think of another question.

She continued. "Yes, she was killed on June 29 on the curve of the dirt road over there. Every year she comes back to that spot, stands on the road, and waits for a car to pick her up. Someone always does. She chats with them until she gets to the end of our driveway and then she leaves them like spirits do. This seems to upset folks when they stop to let her out and she has vanished. Our old friends, who aren't friendly anymore, won't even drive on that road on June 29."

"I, I don't blame them," I admitted too honestly. Goose bumps had established themselves everywhere on my body by now.

"I know. No one comes to see us or wants to have anything to do with us since I brought the spirits here," she complained. "But you have come," she said, brightening, "and I want to give you the spirit."

"No, no, I don't want it," I said stepping away from her. About that time my water arrived from the basement. "I, I don't want that either," I added as I pushed it away.

"You are afraid! AFRAID!" she yelled at me, a sinister look in her eyes. "I'm not going to hurt you nor take your money. You've got $107.38 in your brief case, and I promise I won't touch it. Here, sit down," she urged, taking the chair from the wall and setting it in the middle of the floor.

I needed to sit down-my legs were threatening to drop me. But I wouldn't sit in the middle of the floor. So I grabbed the chair and shoved it against the wall. She would not have that. She pulled it out again. We tussled with that chair back and forth for a bit until I finally slumped into the seat—in the middle of the floor.

"Now," she said in that mysterious, whisper-like voice. "I know who you are. The spirits told me. I will not buy your bocks because the spirit heals all our illnesses; and I have a religion that you should envy. When my husband was dying of heart trouble, I studied spiritualism. Every night some of the neighbor men would come and sit with my husband so I could get some rest. The night I was fully converted and denounced God, the spirits floated right in that bedroom window like sheets of light. But instead of believing, those men took out of here like scared rabbits. Gustov Johnson, my neighbor to the south, was one of them, and he hasn't been back here since. Now you look right into my eyes, and you'll get the spirit."

For some unexplainable reason, I did look into her eyes. The most unusual thing happened. She was standing directly over me with that lifeless, vacant stare, but I saw the whole woman. I saw her from her feet to her head in miniature form, standing as if on air out in the distance. I knew I was being hypnotized or losing control of myself in some other way. I prayed, "God save me."

Immediately I came to my senses, and I saw the witch hovering over me. "You prayed!" she shouted angrily. "You were doing so well too. NOW, LOOK INTO MY EYES."

Almost like a magnet, she drew my eyes back to hers. The scenario was repeated, and I became weaker. I cried, "Oh, God!"

Instantaneously I felt I was back in God's hands. I needed to get out of there, but I was too weak to move. I prayed for God to give me the strength to get out of there. Then I felt energy flow into my arms and legs even as she yelled at me to stop praying. I got up from the chair, grabbed my brief case, and left the house without even so much as a farewell.

When I faced the sunlight again, I was nearly blinded. I had left the place of darkness and demons and had returned to the Son of light. I jumped on my bike and let it coast down the driveway. Turning to the right, I let it coast down the hill to the bridge north of Johnsons' farm. I spent some time by the side of the road thanking God for delivering me from the witch. When I regained my strength, I rode on to Johnsons. When I got there, they were eating their afternoon lunch. They knew by my weak and pallid appearance that I had been at the witch's place.

"Why did you go there?" Mr. Johnson questioned.

"I don't know," I answered. "I guess I didn't realize where I was."

I didn't want to talk about my soul shattering experience with anyone. I simply wanted to block it out of my mind. Now I knew why Mr. Johnson hadn't told me about his experience at the witch's house when the spirits had entered the bedroom window and floated like sheets of light around her sick husband. I knew now that spiritualism was absolutely nothing to ridicule; it is real. The witch had proved her power, a gift of the evil spirits. I never wanted to tangle with it again. I believe that God allowed me to have this experience to help me grow spiritually and to know how to better handle a problem I would have later in life.

Mr. Johnson drove me home to Bird Island that night. The next day Miss Lindsey and I delivered the last of my books for the summer. Miss Lindsey tried to inveigle the witch story from me, but the emotional trauma was still too great. I could only refer to it in general terms—no specifics.

Friday I told Pauline, Miss Lindsey, and Ma and Pa Martin goodbye, and boarded the bus for Colman, South Dakota. Besides my suit case, I carried a box of

MIDGE ON HER OWN

silverware and two small appliances, my extra money, my full scholarship, and lots of wonderful memories of my Minnesota summer adventure.

CHAPTER 14

PRACTICING PROFESSIONALISM

I awakened to the wonderful sounds of an August morning on the farm—sheep bleating, cows mooing, chickens clucking, and Fido barking. I was happy to be home again, resting in the same bed we girls had slept in ever since I could remember. I stretched lazily, remembering that today I didn't have to hurry off to my canvassing territory. I didn't have to meet strangers all day. I really had nothing to do—except—except! Suddenly, I remembered—in three weeks I would be in school again, not as a student but as a teacher! I had a lot to do to get ready for that assignment. There were some things I could do to prepare myself for this position while there was one thing I couldn't change—my looks.

I leaped out of bed and ran to the mirror. Did I look like a teacher? My reflection told me that my hair was a mess, and I didn't look like a teacher. I ran downstairs to mom, gave her a big kiss, and settled into a chair beside her at the breakfast table.

"Mmm, these cinnamon rolls are good," I said as I broke off another one and filled my bowl with corn flakes. "Mom, tell me. Do I look like a professional? I mean, do I look like a teacher?"

Mom looked me over. "No, I can't say that you do." Mom was always bare-faced honest and said it with no prefaces or psychological frills. "Midge, you look more like 16 than 21. You'll need to convince your students that you are their teacher by your decorum. You need to practice being professional."

"But how? I'm kind of scared of this teaching assignment. I wished I hadn't let myself get talked into doing this."

"Midge, don't you know yourself yet? You always let yourself get talked into things. Then you throw yourself—heart and soul—into everything you do, like a timber man at a wood-chopping contest." Mom smiled at her own analogy. "Anyway, you need to be more reserved. Don't talk or act before you think. That's always been one of your problems—you leap before you look. So now, you must look and act like a woman. Carry yourself with dignity, and pretend that you are 30. Then love your kids and know your material. You'll succeed."

"Whee! Sounds like a big assignment," I said, taking a deep breath.

"Well, there are some pluses about your teaching in Sioux Falls this year," Mom said. "You'll be only 33 miles from home, and we hope you can come home every few weeks to see us. Once you get married to a preacher, it's hard telling when we'll see you or where you'll be. At least, we can enjoy you this year."

I helped myself to some of mom's sweet, ever-bearing strawberries, and allowed myself more calories by pouring on thick country cream. "Yes. I thought of that too. Don't look skeptical—I DID! I also thought it would be nice to be close to home while I'm planning my wedding for next summer. Oh, by the way, Wayne will be here in two weeks, OK?"

"Sure it's OK. He's a nice boy and we like him. He fits in with our family. In the meantime…"

"I know, Mom, practice being professional."

PRACTICING PROFESSIONALISM

In late August, Wayne hitchhiked up to Colman and we had a week to spend together. We drove my folks' car to Sioux Falls to find an apartment for me. We answered every ad, but the few we found were dingy basement apartments with broken furniture and a 40-watt light bulb hanging from the ceiling. Catacombs would have been preferable to these places. I imagined such an apartment could depress me.

We decided to visit the Zimmermans for ideas. Margarite and her mother were Adventist friends of my family. Together they ran a very successful potato chip factory in eastern South Dakota. They welcomed us, and we discussed my dilemma. Mrs. Zimmerman suggested, "Why don't you rent a room from us. I'll give you room and board for $30 a month."

"Oh, that would be great!" I said enthusiastically. (Whoops! Remember your dignity. Practice professionalism, I told myself. But such good news deserved a hearty response.)

This proved to be a wonderful arrangement. I felt safe in their home, and my rent, utilities, and food were all included in one monthly payment. When I'd go home on weekends I would take some Zim's Tater Chips for my folks and return with country cream, eggs, and other fresh farm produce for the Zims. Living with Zims was like being with family. They even provided me with all the fresh, crunchy potato chips I wanted to munch at nights while I graded papers.

Another big problem I needed to solve was my transportation to and from school. The bus schedule in my end of town was very erratic. I didn't own a car nor did I have the money to buy one. During the war very few new cars were manufactured; even good used ones were becoming scarce. Furthermore, gasoline rationing put a crimp in everyone's driving habits. But I had to get to school every day.

It was Wayne who came up with a solution. "Midge, I have $150 in the bank. It's my life savings. How much could you scrape up?"

"I have about $50 from my canvassing this summer. Why?" I asked.

"Well, when we get married we'll want a car. So why don't we buy it now and you can use it this year," Wayne suggested.

"Oh, no, Wayne. I couldn't do that," I protested.

"Sure you can. Let's go down to the used car lots and look around."

Before I knew it, we were at a used car lot. Wayne spotted a 1937 two-door Ford that took his fancy. He haggled over the price a bit, and the two men came to an agreement. Wayne and I made a $175 deposit on the car, and I was to make the eight monthly payments of $27.50. It seemed like a crazy thing to do. We weren't married yet, but we had a business agreement. The salesman shook his head, "I hope this works out. Who is responsible if it doesn't? Well, I guess that's your problem. In any case, I need to do a little work on the car. You can come in on Wednesday afternoon to pick it up, Miss Thompson."

The salesman wasn't the only person to shake his head at our arrangement. Our families and friends were equally astonished at our partnership deal.

It was hard for Wayne and I to part again. He went back for his junior year at Union College, and I moved into Zimmerman's home for my year of professionalism.

On Monday morning I unlocked the door to my little one-room school. Wayne and I had fixed it up the week before, so the room was ready. But was I? I wore a long, somber-colored dress and tried to make myself look as old as possible. I even thought about wearing my hair up in a bun—it would make me appear taller, if not older.

Soon my dozen students began to arrive. Bobby, grade seven, and Wesley, grade five, sidled up to me. "You aren't much taller than we are, Miss Thompson."

"That's right. Haven't you heard that good things come in small packages," I responded. "Further, the size of the head has no relation to the number of brain cells functioning therein."

They didn't get the full import of my speech, and neither did I, but at least I confused them. "Whatever does she mean by that?" they asked one another.

Marilyn and Virginia were my giggly, teen-age eighth graders. Edith was in Wesley's class. Perry and Jeannie were sweet little fourth graders. I soon learned to use Francis Nash, a very brilliant third grader, as my helper. Verle, Karen, and Eleanor, second graders, were lovable little darlings having hardly lost their baby fat. Then I had one very shy little first grader, Eloise, who would cry at the slightest provocation. I had every grade to teach except grade six. I had at least six classes to teach each grade per day. That meant 42 lessons to prepare and teach, plus 84 papers to grade per day. The burden seemed almost overwhelming. This job was looking less attractive every minute.

The first morning, I got through only a few lessons before it was time for recess. Believe me, I was ready for recess. The older boys and girls had already begun to smart off a bit. I would show them. They would play ball with me or know the reason why. I was good at soft ball, and I'd teach those kids a thing or two about that game. Wesley and Bobby choose up sides—and left me out. "OK," I said, "that automatically leaves me the pitcher for both sides."

"Oh, no, Miss Thompson," they argued, "the teacher always keeps score."

"I will do both," I assured them as I stood in the pitcher's hole (we weren't sophisticated enough to have a mound—just a depression in the middle of the playing field.) "We'll have the little kids bat first," I said decidedly, wanting my students to know that I was in charge.

I tossed them gentle, straight pitches, and let them strike until they hit the ball. They nearly wore me out before their bat connected with the ball, but their little faces glowed with satisfaction when it happened. Even if they got out at first, it didn't seem to matter. They had hit the ball and that made them feel like real ball players.

When the five older children got up to bat, I winged those balls across the plate as fast as I could. "Three strikes, Virginia," I called. "You're out." I struck out Wesley, Bobby, and Marilyn too. I let Edith hit. Then recess was over. Four very sober older children trooped into the room looking puzzled. This wasn't the pattern their ball games had taken in the past-they had batted and batted while the little kids had chased their balls. How well I knew this routine from my own childhood years when I had attended an all-eight-grade country school. My teacher had let the big kids run us younger ones ragged, and I was going to make sure that didn't happen here.

The rest of the morning passed quietly. During the lunch hour Wesley opined, "Boy, you sure can pitch, Miss Thompson."

"I should," I answered nonchalantly. "I pitched some on the soft ball team in high school."

From the surprised looks that passed from one student to the other I might as well have claimed I played in the major leagues. I could tell they were duly impressed. I wondered what they would tell their parents that night about the way I played with them. "Now," I thought, "if you can just teach as well as you can play ball, you'll do OK, Miss Thompson."

On Wednesday I went to the dealer to pick up our car. "It's all ready," the mechanic assured me as he handed me the keys.

I swelled with pride as I slid behind the wheel and drove out onto the street—Wayne's and my first car. "It's practically new," I reflected contentedly, "only six years old." It handles well too, I thought, as I stopped at the first intersection.

Suddenly, I smelled smoke. Then I noticed it was coming from under the hood and filtering into the car, choking me. I just sat there frozen in my seat. A fireman rushed to me from across the street, carrying a fire extinguisher in his hand. "Out, Miss, OUT!" he shouted as he lifted the car's hood.

Instantly, I yanked on the door handle and tumbled out of the car onto the street. The fireman was soon assisted by others and the fire was out. What good fortune for me that the car caught fire directly across the street from the city's main fire station.

I was still bewildered, "What did I do wrong?"

"Nothing," they assured me. "Whoever worked on this car left an old rag and oil all over the motor. As soon as it got hot, it caught fire."

"Well, I just got it from the Ford garage down the street," I said.

"It's going right back there too," a husky fireman declared. He twisted the steering wheel around and headed my car back down the street while the others pushed.

Not knowing what else to do, I followed them back to the garage.

The garage owner apologized profusely, "Can't get good mechanics these days," he explained. "All the good ones are in the armed services."

The firemen were tough, however, and made the owner promise to do everything except cut off his hands to make things right. Then the owner drove me out to Zimmermans.

I went back on Friday to pick up the car. It worked great! It was cleaned inside and out, with a wax job that lasted a year. Getting to school was easy now that I had a car—no more extended waits for bus service.

In the next few weeks I learned how to make my teaching job easier. I combined classes, used worship periods effectively for problem solving, and told stories for character building. I also discovered that if I held little Eloise on my lap and cuddled her before I asked her to read she could do it. Otherwise she would get nervous and cry. When Eloise ran out of something to do, I let her comb my hair to relax her tensions. One day as she was doing so, she felt all around the back of my head. "What are you doing, Eloise?" I asked.

"I'm looking for the eyes in the back of your head," she said.

"Wha-a-at?" I asked, incredulous.

"Yep," she answered as she continued to lift layers of my thick, curly hair and probe about with her fingers. "The big kids said that you got eyes in the back of your head, and I wanna see 'em. They say that's how you know what we're doin' even when your back is turned."

"So-o-o-o! That's what they say!" I commented as I scanned the crimson faces of my older students. "Perhaps you should tell them that I have good ears too."

The children looked so chagrined that I burst out laughing. Finally they laughed too.

"You know, children, after we have been in school many years, we develop a sixth sense for what is happening around us. But you need not worry about what Eloise told me. I know kids sometimes say funny things about their teachers. But I love you anyway. You are usually good children, and you are making good progress scholastically. I'm pleased to be your teacher. We're going to have a great year together."

They clapped and we hugged. We really did have a great year. I loved those children so much that I almost hated to part with them for weekends. They were glad to see me again on Monday mornings too.

Nearly every weekend that I went home that fall, I took a few of the children with me. It was such fun exposing these city kids to life on the farm. They would talk about their experiences on Miss Thompson's farm for weeks after their visit.

We had other fun times too—parties and school programs. I wrote poems and plays that just suited the age and ability of my students, and they performed with a flare for acting. They made both their parents and me proud of them.

I enjoyed the people of the Sioux Falls church too. I was especially happy that Oscar and Moreen Andersen, Mars and Dick's parents, had moved to town. Our families had always been good friends. By this time, Dick had gone to Omaha and married, and Mars had been drafted into the army. Mars came home on furlough the first two weeks in November. Almost every evening we went out somewhere to a program, ball game, or to a friend's house. We had such fun just being together again like we had at camp meeting and the academy. He really was like a brother to me.

The last night of Mars' furlough we sat on the couch in the living room discussing the future. It was serious talk. We knew his unit might be going overseas. I was naturally concerned for Mars because I knew he had gotten a bit careless spiritually. Then Mars turned to me, took both of my hands in his, and asked, "Shorty, will you marry me?"

"Mars!" I exclaimed incredulously, after I was able to draw a breath. "You shouldn't joke about things like that! What if I would take you seriously?"

"I AM serious," he said, tears surfacing in his eyes. "I've always loved you. But you've always been dating someone else."

"Mars, I am engaged to Wayne."

"Break it."

"I have no intention of breaking it. I love him."

"But you love me too," Mars contended.

"Of course, but not in the same way."

"Then am I too late again?" Mars asked, his hands trembling.

"No. I have always loved you like a brother, and I'm sure it could never have been any different. Mars," I pleaded looking deep into his eyes, "please don't ruin a beautiful friendship with romance."

"Shorty, I need you," Mars begged. "Wayne doesn't. If you married me I know I could be a Christian."

"Don't lay that guilt on me, Mars," I said quietly. "I know you struggle with religion, but being a Christian is not something I can bestow upon you. It's a relationship you have to develop with Jesus. You don't get religion through osmosis. You have to have your own faith and cling to it no matter what. Jesus will help you face disappointments, enemy guns, and anything else the devil throws at you. No one but God is there to hold your hand through trials. No, Mars, I've known of too many people who have asked their marriage partner to help them be Christians. Then when they become angry at the spouse for some reason, they lose their religion too. What kind of loyalty to Christ is that?"

"Then you wouldn't consider marrying me?" Mars asked. Disappointment and pain covered his face. I had never known the jovial, fun-loving, talented Mars to look like this. It made me feel so badly that I wanted to cry. I knew he was hurt, but I also knew we could never marry. I was still shocked that he could even think such a thing.

I shook my head. "No, Mars, I honestly can't marry you. I wish you God's blessings, but we weren't meant to be married."

Then Mars kissed me on the cheek. "Pray for me."

"I will, I most certainly will," I assured him as he hurried out the door.

I never saw Mars alive again. I did pray for him, but his Christian walk was rocky. Only God knows if I will see my friend from my teenage years in heaven. But I know God helped me make the right decision. Marrying Mars would never have assured his salvation. He had to learn to lean upon Christ alone, not upon me. So I closed that chapter of my life.

I really looked forward to seeing Wayne once a month. He hitch-hiked the 200 miles from Lincoln to Sioux Falls faithfully, no matter the weather. Then the time would pass all too quickly, and he would head back to school on Sunday nights.

Thanksgiving and Christmas vacations were longer and gave us time to get better acquainted. It also gave us time to talk about our wedding plans. We decided on a

June wedding until the South Dakota Conference asked me to be the Assistant Colporteur Leader for the summer of 1944. Then we changed the date to August.

The colporteur rally was held at Union College during the month of February. So as a leader, I had to attend and line up student colporteurs for the summer. It hardly seemed possible that only the year before I had been approached by Miss Lindsey and had agreed to become a student colporteur in Minnesota. Now I would be doing for others what she had done for me. I did my job faithfully and signed up five girls to canvass that summer. Of course, I took every opportunity to see Wayne too.

March, with all its changeable weather, was upon us. It was then that my Father and Julius both came down with the mumps at the same time. They had giant-sized cases of this disease. Dad went delirious with his pain and swelling. Mom could not do all of the chores outside by herself. Besides, it was lambing season. They couldn't find a hired man at any price—so many young men were serving in the army that farm work was suffering. In desperation, I called Wayne. "Julius says he'll pay you well if you can get away from school for two weeks and help them on the farm until he can get back on his feet."

"I'll be there by this evening," Wayne said without a moment's hesitation.

I told Julius that Wayne was coming. Julius was so relieved that he slid down further into bed and sighed, "God bless him. He's a saint. A saint, I tell you."

Wayne arrived early that evening, and we finished the chores together. Since it was Sunday night, I had to hurry back to Sioux Falls. I went home each weekend that Wayne was there to see him and check up on the family. Being a country boy himself, Wayne did a superb job. We all missed him when he left, but he had to get back to school. Wayne tucked away the money he earned for our wedding.

During the first week in May, the conference office called and asked me if I would be willing to give my five lady student colporteurs to the regular leader since he had none. Either the young men had to stay in college over the summer or get drafted. I gladly gave up that job and called Wayne.

When I relayed the message to him, he was elated. "Good! Let's get married June 18. I have a break between summer school sessions then."

"Wait a minute," I said trying to edge in a reasonable word.

But Wayne went on, "I have from Thursday night to Monday morning off."

"But that's not much time," I protested. "I'd hardly call that a break. Besides, I can't get things ready that soon. I don't have my wedding dress sewn nor my going-away outfit..."

"What going-away outfit?" he laughed. "We won't be going anywhere with this gas rationing. Besides, I have to get back to college."

"But I don't have time to do anything between now and when school is out. There are just three weeks between school closing and June 18. I don't think I can be ready that soon."

"All right. You set the date, but I can't likely get up there before the first of August then. And I feel very strongly that I should be there for our wedding."

We both laughed. "GI's are getting married over the phone every day," I teased. "But seriously, I'll consider June 18."

"I love you lots, Honey. I can't wait to have you here in Lincoln with me. But please make up your mind in time so I can notify my parents. They'd like to come to my wedding—they never got to the weddings of my two brothers nor sister Fern's."

"I'll let you know real soon. Like now. Let's plan on June 18."

There was an explosion on the other end of the line. "Praise the Lord! I got to go tell the guys. Goodbye."

The next few weeks were extremely busy for me. I shopped in town for a going-away outfit. I found something that was practical and at a price I could afford. I got a navy-blue-and-white dress, white hat, purse, and shoes. These I could wear all summer. I finished the school year off with a graduation program for Marilyn and Virginia in which all of the other children took part. I sent in my reports to the county and to the conference. The children helped me put away books and clean the desks. Then they left, and I was alone. Nine months had passed all too quickly. I sat at my desk and surveyed the room.

As my eye passed from one desk to another, I thought of each child who had been its occupant. Some had come from loving Christian homes, some from broken homes, and one from almost no home at all. Whatever the circumstances of their home life, I had tried to make school a comfortable, secure, and loving place for them. My heart ached for the one child who almost never had a lunch. Mrs. Zimmerman made him her missionary project and packed a daily lunch for him that was fit for a king. When he got to school each morning, he would grab that lunch, run to the church basement, and devour part of it. And I let him do it. I surmised that the lunch served as his breakfast too.

PRACTICING PROFESSIONALISM

Everyone has good and bad days, and so it was with my children. I had tried to help them through those times. I laughed with them and cried with them. I had gotten emotionally involved with them. I had learned much about people and life and work that year; I would be forever indebted to the people of the Sioux Falls church. I cried as I picked up my things and turned the key in the school door for the last time.

I could have spent quite a melancholy evening had it not been for the church and school picnic that had been planned for that Thursday evening. So I hurried out to the park where everyone had gathered. I discovered then that the picnic was a farewell and bridal shower in my honor. How appropriate that my children could share with the church in this occasion! The church people gave me some wonderful gifts, but the nicest gift of all was the one given me by church school parents and children—a lovely set of China covered with a pink rose pattern.

My older girls had been so excited about my wedding that I shared some of my plans with them and showed them things in my trousseau including my rose-engraved silverware. With this in mind, they had helped shop for the dishes which were a perfect match for my silver. Their faces shone with pride when they saw how pleased I was with their gift.

We ended the evening by singing, "Blest be the tie that binds, our hearts in Christian love." Then, whether it was professional or not, I couldn't resist reaching out to the dozen children who had latched themselves onto my heart. They flocked to me, and we huddled together. With hugs and tears we parted. I felt the force of Christian love and knew now what it meant to belong to the family of God.

Church School—Sioux Falls, South Dakota, 1943–44.

CHAPTER 15

1 + 1 = 1

"I'm home, Mom," I yelled as I burst through the door.

"Good!" Mom said, hugging and kissing me. "I've been waiting for you. First, there is this package from your sister Dorathy."

"Oh, I know what it is!" I squealed. I tore open the package and spilled its contents onto the dining room table. "Oh, Mom, isn't this the most gorgeous satin and lace you have ever seen? Dorathy has always been so sweet to me. Imagine! Sending me the material for my wedding dress! Now, I can't wait to start sewing it."

"It's absolutely beautiful!" Mom agreed, fingering the satin gently.

"Well, I'll sew that in the evenings," I said trying to control my excitement. "Now, Mom, what do you want me to do for you in the next three weeks and two days before my wedding.?"

"Paint the ceilings and walls of the living room, dining room, and kitchen and the steps to the second floor and paper my downstairs bedroom," She said without even taking a breath. "That's my master plan."

"Wow! That's quite an assignment!" I exclaimed. "Mom, do you know you are a real slave driver? I'll probably be too old to get married by the time I get all of that done. Besides did you remember that I'm Midge, not Goliath?"

"What do you mean by that?" Mom questioned.

"Well, the ceilings are high, and I am short," I explained. "Do you have a good arm stretcher? Even a step ladder might be helpful."

"I've got a step ladder." She looked at me seriously. Mom never did get our little jokes. Dad always had to explain them to her. "Now I don't know if you can get all of that work done before your wedding or not. But what you don't get done probably won't get done for awhile. Dad and I can't do that kind of work anymore, and Julius is too busy in the fields. I tried to hire someone to do it but that's impossible—everyone is so involved in the war effort. I wanted the house to look real nice for your sisters when they come."

"Yep! They'll all be here for the family reunion and my wedding except Martena. By the way, your nursery-size flower beds make the lawn look Edenic."

"Thanks," mother smiled. "We'll set up picnic tables out in the lawn to siphon some of the crowd away from the dining room during meal time."

"Good idea. Did you know that Wayne's folks are coming too?"

"Yes, they wrote to me. They'll get here Thursday before the wedding. Oh, there's so much to do," Mom sighed. "I do hope we can get it all done."

"Don't worry; I'll get it done. I just don't want you to wear yourself out so you can't enjoy my wedding with me. In the past you've been the Martha, cooking for crowds and serving them. This time, your daughters have decided that you will relax and enjoy yourself. Once they get here, they're taking over. You will be assigned a rocking chair where you will sit and chat with your children, one at a time."

Mom looked shocked. "You mean they'll kick me out of my own kitchen?"

1 + 1 = 1

"Exactly! But in the meantime you have to cook for Dad, Julius, and your slave—me. And it had better be good!" I teased.

Mom nodded and took me out to the entry way. She showed me the buckets of paint she had already purchased in faith that I would get the work done.

I started painting Sunday morning. During the next two weeks my muscles complained constantly that they belonged to a teacher—not a painter. There were four good results from the strain: 1) The house sparkled. 2) Mom was pleased. 3) I slept soundly. 4) I lost ten pounds.

My sister Dorathy arrived from California the week before the wedding. She was a big help. She completed the rest of mom's house fixing goals by painting the steps, washing and waxing the floors, and preparing all the beds. That released me to finish sewing my wedding dress and a dress for Mom.

On Wednesday the excitement escalated. Family began to arrive from everywhere. Gladys, Jean, and her four-year old, Lois, came from Idaho. Lela, Ray, and baby Jerry drove up from Kansas.

Wayne came in from Lincoln on Thursday, and his parents came by train from Oregon the same night. Now the house was bulging with people, and my parents were in their glory.

On Friday Wayne and I had to go to Flandreau to get our marriage license. Both sets of parents went with us. (My sisters had indeed evicted Mom from her kitchen and taken over.) It was a good thing the Olsons were with us. Wayne lacked four months from being 21 years old. Such being the case, South Dakota law required his parents' signature.

Wayne was miffed. "You mean I can be drafted without my parents consent, but I can't get married without it?"

"Right," the clerk answered, a bit embarrassed by the apparent incongruity.

After securing our license, we stopped to pick up some more flower-girl dress material. Since I had been a flower girl for my sister Jean's wedding, we all thought it would be special to have her daughter, Lois, be a flower girl for my wedding. I had already asked Twyla Ochenga, the daughter of my childhood friend Wanda Scriven, to be a flower girl. Her dress was sewn, but Lois' would have to be a hurry-up job.

On Saturday night Jean and I cut and sewed Lois' dress. On Sunday Lela, Ray, Gladys, Julius, Wayne and I decorated the little white church on the country hillside with the most available flowers from our yard—peonies. Their sweet aroma filled the church. Then DeEtta Knect Olson came to play the organ while we practiced marching. Lois and Twyla took their job seriously, dropping individual peony petals. When we all felt confident of the program, we went back to the house and ate a picnic lunch on the lawn. Goldie Webber, my academy roommate, joined us. She had come from Sioux Falls by bus bringing my wedding bouquet of red roses.

Then everyone dressed for the wedding and left for the church. Mom, Dad, and I were left alone. Mom looked pretty in her new dress. Dad, accustomed to overalls, looked uncomfortable in his suit and tie. Then as they looked at me, their youngest child, dressed for her wedding, I noted tears in their eyes. Joy, pride, sadness? I wasn't sure.

"It isn't easy for Mom and me to see you leave the nest and build your own, Middy," Dad said, clearing his

1 + 1 = 1

throat to get control of his voice. "But Wayne is a mighty nice boy, and we trust you two will have a happy home."

Dad sparked nostalgic emotion in me with this little speech. But this was not the time for tears, so we quickly hopped into the Chevy coupe and rode to the church. Then Mom and Dad went into the church, leaving me alone in the car. Suddenly, I got nervous. Was I doing the right thing? Did I really love Wayne enough to live with him forever? I looked at the keys left in the ignition. I could easily drive myself away from all of this. For a moment I was tempted; then I remembered that I had come to this decision after much prayer. God had seemed to smile His approval on our union, so I had better go through with it.

I opened the door of the car and walked deliberately to the entry way of the church. Lela and Ray, our attendants, and the minister had already taken their places on the platform. The coordinator was trying to get the flower girls to do their thing, but Twyla balked. "I'm not going—there's a bad man in there!" she cried, pointing at a bewhiskered man on the back pew.

Nothing could persuade her otherwise. Fortunately, Lois didn't care who was in there, so intent was she on dropping her petals.

With a smile on his face, but a tear in his eye, Dad tucked my arm in his, and we were on our way down the aisle. Gladys sang as beautifully as always, and DeEtta was absolute perfection on the old pump organ. Elder Reed gave us the usual instruction, and concluded with, "What God hath joined together, let no man put asunder." I smiled to myself, remembering my childhood understanding of that text—let no man put US under. Before I got the grin off my face, it was time for the groom to kiss the bride. Wayne Olson and Mildred Thompson were now joined together as ONE. Strange mathematics isn't it? The Bible says that one man married to one woman makes ONE—"The two shall be one flesh."

Though that may be true symbolically, literally they occupy two spaces and eat from two plates. And one plus one cannot live as cheaply as ONE. We would pay for two from now on, but there would be two of us to do it.

We left the church directly because everyone came to our house for the evening meal. Besides the mounds of food that my sisters had prepared, the neighbors and friends brought in more. Everybody ate of the abundance while Wayne and I circulated among the crowd, speaking to each guest. When we had completed the rounds, I changed into my navy blue going-away outfit. Then we ate. I don't know what we ate, but Wayne made a good impression on the cooks by packing away quite a bit. Then we cut the cake, Dorothy and Jean served it, and Julius scooped out gallons of ice cream. I liked the dairy fresh ice cream, and I remember I ate some of it. In fact, I handed Julius my bowl for a second helping. To him, that seemed perfectly normal—I always had seconds on ice cream. But Wayne and I had a plan to escape the country fun-makers. I set my bowl down on the sink when no one was watching, and we ran to Dad's car. As we slid into the front seat, we heard someone yell, "They've gone. Into your cars, gang!"

Dad had parked his car for our convenience at the end of the driveway. Wayne started the motor and drove away quietly with no lights until we got to the first intersection at the bottom of the hill. By then we could see the headlights of other cars pulling out of my parent's driveway, but they were too late. We escaped to the farm home of Julia and Chris Jokumsen where we would spend the night. We were already undressed and studying our Sabbath School lesson when the gang caught up with us. They had tried the motels and didn't find us. So by deduction, they figured out where we might be. About a dozen people came tramping up the stairs, clapping and singing discordant music. They sat around and chatted for awhile, then tripped gaily away, taking our shoes.

It wasn't a catastrophe to be left without shoes for the night. Julia had invited my whole family and the Olsons over to her house for a wedding breakfast brunch. Mom came bringing our shoes; she was still pretty mad at the intruders who had taken them. "Yah," she said, "they came back bragging about their fun. I let them know how dumb and thoughtless they were. I told them Midge was very tired after three weeks of painting, and Wayne had only a few days respite from school. I told them a lot more too and made those hayseeds feel ashamed."

"She surely did!" Lela whispered to me on the side, grinning. "Remember how Mom can scold? Well, she hasn't lost that ability."

After brunch, we all went to the photographer to get both wedding and family pictures taken. We got home in time for a late afternoon lunch, then went out to look at what they had done to our car. They had really fixed it up. They had removed the bucket seat on the passenger's side, and had replaced it with a toilet stool. They had set a small coup with a live mother hen and baby chicks on the back seat. Since tires were at a premium, they didn't touch them, but they chained the back axle to Dad's farm tractor. We couldn't have gone anywhere with that car. We had a good laugh, took some snapshots of the car inside and out, and then my family helped restore it to normal. The worst part was scrubbing the white calcimined "Just Married" off the black car.

Later that evening, my sisters packed our wedding gifts and put them in the back seat and trunk of our

Ford. In the morning, Wayne and his parents drove to Lincoln. Since my sisters had come so far for the family reunion and my wedding, it was decided that I should spend some time at home with them. This was nice, but, inwardly, I was anxious to go to Lincoln and be with Wayne.

Thursday evening Wayne and his parents met me at the bus depot, and we drove to the apartment—our first home. I made a quick inspection of the quarters. It had a midget-sized kitchen with a cute little breakfast nook at one end. The living room, bedroom, and bath room were all commodious. I was elated. Wayne had done a good job in choosing our apartment.

Wayne's folks left for Kansas the next week. Wayne was already back in summer school, so I looked for work. I found employment in a local grocery store at the meat department. I knew nothing at all about cuts of meat and hated to handle the stuff. It was good pay, however, and I could buy my groceries there at a discount. They didn't sell pork at all, and the manager cut the meat. I only had to package it for the customers.

Wayne worked a few hours each day helping the builders with the new science complex. Between our work and my Minnesota scholarship we did very well financially. Our food, rent, books, and tuition was easily covered. Wayne's parents had given us $400 as a wedding present, and we bought a used piano. Wayne thought that I, as a minister's wife, should know how to play the piano. I took six lessons—enough for the basics. Then I practiced on my own, though I still played better by ear.

Our year at Lincoln was a lot of fun. There were many married couples at school that year and our Married Couples Club sponsored more activities than other college organizations.

1 + 1 = 1

Martena and her family moved to Lincoln that year too. Her husband Marvin took the pre-dental course, and she took some more education courses. Sometimes I baby-sat their children—Marlin, Joyce, and Darlene—while their parents worked or studied. It was very nice having relatives living within a block of us.

Wayne gained weight that year—which was quite remarkable since he was living on my cooking. Either I was doing something right or those peanut butter sandwiches and breakfast food had an awful lot of calories. Fortunately I learned how to operate a can opener and turn on the gas. Wayne was a good sport through all my learning experiences and burnt offerings. Once in awhile he'd scrutinize a casserole dish I concocted and ask, "What's that?" Admittedly it wasn't like his Mom's cooking or even cafeteria food, but he survived.

Halfway through the year, I got the mumps. I mean, I was Mrs. Chipmunk with extra padding in her jowls. I ran such a high fever that I became delirious. One day as Wayne sat cross-legged on my bed in his short pajamas, I looked down and noticed the white skin covering his leg from the ankle to his knee. In my delirium, I thought I was in the store looking at a roll of liverwurst. I pointed at his leg and asked, "Do you want it sliced or in chunks."

"Whoa!" he exclaimed. "That's my leg you're talking about. I want it whole!" When Wayne realized I was sick enough to hallucinate, he called a doctor. I've wondered since how he decided which kind of doctor to call—one for the head or the body.

In March, Wayne got a letter from the Kansas Conference asking him to work there as a ministerial intern. We were very pleased to know that upon graduation he had a call to work as a minister. I got a call too. The Nebraska Conference invited me to be their assistant field secretary for the summer, but the Kansas Conference objected—"When we hire a man, his wife comes with him."

During the Foreign Mission Institute, Elder E. E. Cossentine, the college president, took Wayne and me aside. "Have you volunteered for foreign mission service yet?" he asked.

"No, but we'd be willing to go as a missionaries," Wayne answered.

"Well, I've already recommended you. Go when the call comes. Don't disappoint me," Elder Cossentine said.

It was a special serendipity to know the college president felt that we were worthy of foreign mission service. We would not disappoint him or God if the call came.

Spring came and we surrendered our Pathfinder responsibilities quite gladly. Everyone should experience that work of the church sometime in their life — once — especially if their nerves are well insulated.

My mother came down for Wayne's graduation. He was the only graduate that I saw—perhaps there were others. They said there were 50 in his class.

Then we bought a trailer, packed it with our possessions, and headed for our ministerial work in the Pittsburgh-Fort Scott, Kansas, area. I was sorry to have to sell and leave behind our one prize possession. We couldn't get our lovely piano into the little trailer.

Elder McWilliams, our mentor, welcomed us to his district of five churches. "You will preach at two churches every Sabbath, and I'll take two," he instructed. "Now find yourself a house in Fort Scott as soon as possible. We'll be starting an effort in two weeks."

We hunted all over the small town for housing. There simply was none. Finally, down a dirt road on the

1 + 1 = 1

Our house was air-conditioned—we could see through the walls. We cooked twice a week at Eld. Williams or on the pavement 1 block away on a paved street.

outskirts of town we found a very run-down house with a "FOR RENT" sign on the outside. What was our pleasure when we finally found the owner and discovered it was also furnished. The rent was right—just $10 per month. But once we looked inside, we discovered that the words "house" and "furniture" were deceptive terms. The house sat on bare ground; the termites had gotten to it before the Orkin Man. Because the underneath supports were eaten away, we could walk only around the edges of the living room safely. One day I tried to take a short cut across the sagging floor and broke through a board. With difficulty, I finally extracted my injured foot. After that, I remembered to take the circuitous route. I regretted making that hole in the floor for three reasons—rats, mice, and snakes. They liked the convenient passageway into our house. I never walked anywhere in the house after that without a light and Wayne. Even then, I panicked every time I saw a moving creature. Wayne became pretty skillful at killing the copper-heads, garter snakes, and rattle snakes, but he seldom got a mouse or rat.

I threw a blanket across the hopelessly soiled davenport and swept off the chair. That made them somewhat usable. The bed sagged like a hammock, but we were young, and our backs were strong. I loved the antique dresser in the bedroom and dusted it faithfully.

Now the kitchen was something else. The kerosene stove could not produce enough heat to cook things like beans or potatoes. Fortunately, I had mastered the use of a can opener. I could fry an egg and boil quick cooking oatmeal in 15 minutes, and warm up a can of soup or vegetables in about 10. We gladly accepted dinner/supper invitations from the McWilliams, Piersons, Eppels and other church members. It was so good to have food that didn't come out of a can.

We did not have a bathroom either. We set water in the sun to warm and took spit-baths. Our outdoor privy leaned precariously to one side, and through the cracks in the door we could watch the traffic go by. Fortunately, very few people lived in our area—the other side of shantytown. We might have rented better quarters had the conference informed us about housing allowance and salary advance. In our ignorance, we saved them money.

"Wayne," I complained one very hot day, "this is ridiculous, living in a house like this. It's too hot to sleep at nights, and we can't use a fan because it blows the fuses. We have to find another house."

"I know," Wayne said as he drew me to him and kissed me. "You've been a good sport about this housing. It really is awful!"

1 + 1 = 1

"Yep! Terrible, trashy! I couldn't endure it if it were not for the wonderful church members and our Bible study interests. I hope God will find better housing for us before winter comes."

And He did—in a very special way.

In August we got a letter from the General Conference Mission Board asking us to join a German class starting in September in preparation for overseas service. I was so thrilled and excited that I almost made the fatal mistake of running across the living room floor. "Oh, Wayne," I exclaimed, suspended somewhere between earth and heaven, "my childhood dreams have been realized! I'm going to be a missionary!! We're going to be missionaries!!!"

Then we knelt by that old beat-up davenport and dedicated our lives to mission service.

This photo was taken to go with Midge and Wayne's application for mission service.

TEACH Services, Inc.
P U B L I S H I N G

We invite you to view the complete
selection of titles we publish at:
www.TEACHServices.com

We encourage you to write us
with your thoughts about this,
or any other book we publish at:
info@TEACHServices.com

TEACH Services' titles may be purchased in
bulk quantities for educational, fund-raising,
business, or promotional use.
bulksales@TEACHServices.com

Finally, if you are interested in seeing
your own book in print, please contact us at:
publishing@TEACHServices.com

We are happy to review your manuscript at no charge.

www.ingramcontent.com/pod-product-compliance
Lightning Source LLC
Chambersburg PA
CBHW070755100426
42742CB00012B/2145